The Civilization of the American Indian Series

BEYOND THE VISION

BEYOND THE VISION

ESSAYS ON AMERICAN INDIAN CULTURE

William K. Powers

University of Oklahoma Press : Norman and London

By William K. Powers

Indians of the Northern Plains (New York, 1969)
Indians of the Southern Plains (New York, 1971)
Oglala Religion (Lincoln, Nebr., 1977)
Yuwipi: Vision and Experience in Oglala Ritual (Lincoln, Nebr., 1982)
Sacred Language: The Nature of Supernatural Discourse in Lakota (Norman, 1986)
Beyond the Vision: Essays on American Indian Culture (Norman, 1987)

Library of Congress Cataloging-in-Publication Data

Powers, William K.
   Beyond the vision.

   (The Civilization of the American Indian series;
v. 184)
   Bibliography: p. 181.
   Includes index.
   1. Indians of North America.   2. Indians of
North America—Religion and mythology.   I. Title.
II. Series.
E77.2.P68   1987   973'.0497   87–40218
ISBN 0–8061–2091–6 (alk. paper)

The paper in this book meets the guidelines for permanence and durability of the Committee on Production Guidelines for Book Longevity of the Council on Library Resources, Inc.

Copyright © 1987 by the University of Oklahoma Press, Norman, Publishing Division of the University. Manufactured in the U.S.A. First edition.

To
Claude Lévi-Strauss

CONTENTS

ILLUSTRATIONS

PREFACE

THE following essays were written and presented to various audiences between 1975 and 1984. Only chapter 3 has been previously published. The thread that ties the chapters together is that they are all about various aspects of American Indian culture.

The book is dedicated to Claude Lévi-Strauss, which is my way of emphasizing his profound influence on my own work, as well as on the general field of American Indian ethnology. And although some of my previous works[1] are decidedly structuralist in their approach, the chapters presented here represent a number of different approaches. Structuralism, as a theory and method, has always appealed to me as the perfect lens through which to view human behavior. But it is also my conviction that singular points of view—and this would include structuralism, if it were relied upon as a singular method of analysis—frequently tend to obscure rather than elucidate what we know or what we might want to learn about culture and society. Lévi-Strauss's nature-culture dyad is metaphorically just as applicable to academic departments and intellectual schools of thought as it is to the understanding of cultural transformations and human evolution. For example, in anthropology a battle still rages over the separation of biological anthropology (nature) from cultural anthropology (culture) instead of these being regarded as parts of a continuum. And more time is spent—or wasted—today over arguing about which school of thought is more accurate or precise than in trying to understand the cultures and societies that these disparate schools of thought purport to describe and explain. Thus, in keeping with my own intent to view humanity through a prism of theories and methods, not just a single one, each following chapter employs several theoretical or methodological frameworks.

The image of a prism is perhaps the proper metaphor for these variegated approaches, and this is where structuralism emerges, to my way of thinking, as an appropriate catalyst to illuminate human behavior. Structuralism is at once a theory and a method, and its boldness permits brave souls to make discoveries that otherwise might have been clouded over by less fruitful approaches. But structuralism does not necessarily preempt these other approaches. Rather it is a guide that helps and prods one along unsure footpaths over narrow, winding mountainous trails. Despite all arguments against structuralism, particularly in the United States, where it is frequently regarded as too capricious, too circumstantial, too contrived for the "serious" scholar, it has made a profound and indelible mark on nearly every humanistic and social science discipline in the universities. And this impression will be perennial because of structuralism's uncanny predilection for turning on itself. This is to say that the same structural methods different disciplines employ to analyze their respective problems in, say, anthropology, art, psychology, or literature, may be used to understand the nature of these disciplines. Thus structural method is useful in understanding similarities and differences among schools of thought as it is in understanding similarities and differences among other "tribes" of humans.

After all, structuralism bases its fundamental principles on its ability to focus on returning patterns and in a sense match those patterns with others of the same sort. This simplistic definition could apply to almost any discipline in the natural sciences, the social sciences, and the humanities, which are themselves related in one of the most common structuralist patterns, that of the dialectic, with social sciences mediating neatly between the humanities and the natural sciences.

One could risk the temptation to be even more simplistic and argue that every discipline that attempts some form of analysis is in fact structural. But the truth of the matter is that, simplistic or not, when one speaks of structuralism positively or negatively, it is impossible to do so without considering that special brand of structuralism that is incontrovertibly linked with the name Claude Lévi-Strauss.[2] Probably, if Lévi-Strauss's name were separated from structural studies, there would not be such an uproar when his name is mentioned among American academics. This is because he is bold and speculative, scientific and philosophical, theoretical and empirical, witty and imaginative, intense and demanding, tedious and exhausting. And clever. But be this as it may, aside from the arguments for and against Lévi-Straussian structuralism, another singular fact throughout all the rage and uproar, frustration, and consternation, goes unnoticed. The fact is: he is an American Indianist who has analyzed more data relevant to American Indian myth, ritual, social organization, and social structure than most other Americanists. Lévi-Strauss is more knowledgeable about the historical, cultural, and ethnological literature, than most native students of American Indian cultures. One rarely thinks of Lévi-Strauss as an American Indianist (I do not know if he considers himself one). His accomplishments in understanding American Indian culture are amazing, if not enviable, but for the most part considered second hand to his "structural" interests.

Without intending to be presumptuous, I rather suspect that in some mythological other life Lévi-Strauss would have made a fine Jesuit missionary whose task it was to learn a primitive culture for the purpose of transforming one set of ideas on religion (that of the people being studied) into another (that of those doing the studying and of course ultimately writing books about their discoveries). Lévi-Strauss's global approach to problems of ethnography remind me very much of the Reverend Eugene Buechel, S.J., the German Jesuit who made a reputation on the Pine Ridge and Rosebud reservations as a linguist par excellence.[3] His job, as it were, was to learn the Lakota language well enough to translate the usual missals, bible, and psalms, and ultimately to write a grammar and dictionary. He did all of the above in his lifetime except the last: the dictionary was published posthumously.

The point of comparison here is that the old Jesuit in his linguistic pursuits, just like Lévi-Strauss in his ethnographic investigations, had to learn a number of other disciplines in order to make sense out of what one could have construed only as nonsense. Father Buechel became a botanist when it was time to collect his entries on plants and herbal medicines; a mammologist when he investigated the animal world of the Lakota; an ornithologist when studying birds; an astronomer when eliciting information on the Lakota heavens, and so on and so on. One might say that the priest became even an anthropologist when it was his interest to learn more about the kinship and social and political organization of the Oglala and Sicangu people with whom he worked.

Lévi-Strauss's multitudinous interest in art, music, drama, myth and ritual, and the ecology of mythology also gives him an uncanny understanding and perspective on the peoples he studies, and these interests manifest themselves through all of his writing perhaps most conspicuously in his works on classification and mythology. This ecological explanation, or what he calls the science of the concrete, makes structuralism all the more appealing for persons who study American Indians. Native Americans in many ways agree naturally with many of the principles of structural methodology and theory, more than with any other school of thought. It has been sometimes difficult in my own work really to differentiate between structural analysis, and what the Lakota—without benefit of training in structuralism or anthropology—treat as their own native exegesis of their cultural behaviors. They perhaps will not agree with Lévi-Strauss or other structuralists on the utility of the nature-culture dyad as it is used most frequently in structural analysis. The Lakota would however agree with the concept, but the components would be arranged so as to include themselves in the "natural" part of the dyad, where white people and modern technology would be placed perhaps on the "cultural" side. It is obvious that other analytical features of structuralism such as binary oppositions exist empirically in Lakota thought and philosophy, and it would be quite accurate to say that in their explanations of culture in their own language they perceive the world very much as a structuralist does. I have discussed some of these aspects of structuralism with people at Pine Ridge, and they are usually quite surprised that any of these structural principles might be regarded as controversial when in fact they are, in Lakota philosophy, an accurate description of the way the universe works.[4]

But, as I have said earlier, a single approach to a cultural phenomenon, and that includes a structural approach, may not be rewarding. The prismatic approach leaves the possibility for integrating more than one theory or method to help explain the facts under study. At once then, structuralism, functionalism, history, symbolism, and evolutionary theory are all compatible and not mutually exclusive categories of analysis.

Chapter 1 reflects my interests in structuralism, evolution, linguistics, and sociobiology, certain combinations of which are traditionally regarded as unlikely bedfellows. I focus on the vocable, heretofore a term applied by ethnomusicologists to nonsemantic utterances found in song, often called meaningless syllables or burden syllables. Although vocables are historically assigned to "primitive" music, I demonstrate that they are found in all music throughout the world and as such are useful in understanding the structure of song and shed some speculative light on the relationship between speech and song. My presentation is in three parts: the first deals with the structure of vocabalic music on the Northern and Southern Plains; the second with the structure and function of vocables; and finally, I address how the understanding of structure and function of vocables may elucidate the origin and development of speech and song. Using Darwinian theories of sexual selection, some of which have become a basis for sociobiological theory, I opt for vocables serving in a midway position between song and speech. The arguments presented in this paper have drawn—expectedly—mixed criticisms from audiences. The greatest detractors are ethnomusicologists who do not give serious thought to theories related to the origin and development of music.[5]

This may owe to the fact that anthropology, with little exception, has never really caught hold in ethnomusicology as it might have. Even today one can attend ethnomusicology meetings and hear outdated theories related to the old *kulturkreiselehr* school presented as support for ideas about "primitive" music. Since the discipline draws heavily from "art" music such as vocal and instrumental traditions of peoples who are musically literate, as well as from music educators, it is understandable that much anthropological theory simply does not fit or matter in the programs and journal articles. The younger generation of ethnomusicologists, heavily influenced by folklore, has concentrated on musical idioms such as jazz, country-western, blues, folk, and pop, all of which are deserving of ethnomusicological analysis. Some diehards still follow in the inspirational footsteps of those forbears who studied "tribal" music, but their expertise lies mainly in their musicological sophistication rather than in their ethnographic abilities. Ethnomusicology, in fact, has struggled for the past twenty-five years to achieve a kind of distinct identity, but unfortunately its methods and theories are frequently not acceptable to either anthropology or musicology.[6]

Chapter 2 is straightforwardly influenced by the work of Dell H. Hymes and the field of sociolinguistics.[7] My objective here is to explain in terms of communications theory just how one group of people, the Oglala of Pine Ridge, South Dakota (and by inference other American Indian populations) regulate their dances. By regulation I mean how dancers know when to start dancing to a song, how long the dance will continue, and when it will end. Of course, the question may be applied to any population, who, as most of us know, can participate fully in its dance culture without ever having to ask these questions.

The solution to the problem of regulation is approached from the combined musical and dance behavior of the singers and dancers who perform at a powwow. Admittedly, the analysis requires a particular sophisticated knowledge of the rules and regulations governing Oglala powwow protocol that does not come easily to the casual observer. My own insights are derived from a lifetime of participation in Lakota culture, as well as in the dance and music culture of other tribes in Oklahoma. Some of the nuances of the paper probably could not have been detected without having an intimate knowledge of the Oglala dance world. As someone who has danced Indian since age nine, I feel quite comfortable in integrating my personal knowledge into an essentially methodological paper, and I see it as a contribution to event analysis, applying sociolinguistic theory to kinesic behavior.[8]

Chapter 3 is about sacred numbers, a phenomenon found in all parts of the world. First presented as part of a symposium on neurobiology, this chapter addresses itself to the manner in which people employ sets of numbers to structure their perceptions of reality. Here sets of numbers rather than singular integers become an important consideration. Drawing upon earlier works of Lucien Lévy-Bruhl, I argue that what is important in Lakota religion is not so much the distinct use of the sacred numbers four and seven as the relationships formed by these two numbers. Further along I compare some ideas from the use of 3 and 4 in Christianity with the Lakota model, suggesting that these numerical sets, although traditionally seen as part of a symbolic system, are equally analyzable as part of a ritual system, since people frequently act out ritual events structured in part by predetermined numerical patterns. If numbers then can be seen as a form of ritual event, the acting out of sacred numbers may in fact have some effect on the equilibration of the two hemispheres of the brain. The theories here combine semiotic structuralism on the one hand and biogenetic structuralism on the other, and as such the chapter argues to unite (or perhaps rejoin) domains nowadays distinguished as biological and cultural anthropology.[9]

In chapter 4, I enter the ongoing debate about the difference between art writ large (with a capital A) and art assigned to the remainder of the world, wherever art is called "primitive." My position, to judge from the title, is not surprisingly structural, but it is a kind of pragmatic structuralism in which I see the same kind of structure underlying both that which is acceptable as *Art* and that which is rarely acceptable as art. As for the pragmatics, I offer what might be called a functional checklist of those elements that emphasize similarities rather than differences, a posture that links structuralism very much to biosocial anthropology; that is, combines according to different methodologies those elements that underscore the similarities rather than differences between people. The emphasis on differences owes largely to those disciplines whose proponents propose that the culture concept has a yet undiscovered empirical reality, rather than seeing it as a complex analytical frame designed for the purpose of comparing cultures. This is not to detract from the utility of the culture concept. If, however, the perceived reality of Culture is momentarily dispensed with, it is more difficult to erect barriers between various anthropological schools of thought. Problems of cultural uniqueness are not of course in the exclusive domain of anthropology. Art history, history, and sociology all suffer form the same malady: a concentration on perceived differences rather than empirical similarities.[10]

Chapter 5 deals with the problem of how people around the world are quite capable of participating in more than one religion simultaneously. The chapter locates certain structural principles in a historical frame. The area studied is the Pine Ridge Reservation, and what I demonstrate is that various nomadic bands, once they were required to settle permanently on the reservation, became structurally and functionally replaced by various Christian denominations. From a sociological point of view, people were able to maintain exogamous band principles that governed marriage. On the surface, people owed allegiance to denominations now rather than bands, but in effect the transformation from band to church allowed the people to maintain continuity in their marriage system.

There were other benefits in becoming nominal Christians while at the same time maintaining a belief in Oglala metaphysics. It was economically beneficial to be Christian, and certainly, from a political point of view, much safer. But when it came time to confront life crises, most Indians sought out a medicine man for spiritual direction. Although the combina-

tion of traditional Lakota values along with Christian ethics
has been described by others as simply another example of
religious "syncretism," I argue that it is the nature of culture
to be syncretic; therefore, syncretism as an analytical term is
useless.

Chapter 6 seeks to compare some aspects of psychiatry as
practiced in middle-class America with ritual curing under
the supervision of a modern-day medicine man. There has
been a long relationship between psychiatry, psychology, and
anthropology, and this chapter places both types of ritual
practitioners on a more equal footing. As it is true in art and
religion that certain exotic terms such as "shaman" have been
used to identify those customs and practices associated with
"primitive" peoples, I argue that the mere use of such terms
automatically gives their practitioners an inferior status. The
comparison of two culturally different types of curing (at least
on the surface) again has some pragmatic objectives. Much of
contemporary psychiatric curing is done under the auspices
of the Public Health Service at Pine Ridge. I try to underscore
what I see as fundamental differences between psychiatry
and ritual curing by medicine men from the Indians' point of
view, and I hope that it will make some small contribution to a
better understanding of health at Pine Ridge as well as to
other points of intersection between ritual practitioners of
culturally disparate peoples.[11]

Finally, in chapter 7, I address the issue of the overwhelming influences that American Indian religion has had on non-
Indian America as well as on other parts of the world, especially Europe. This essay is essentially an ethnography of
Euro-American attitudes about American Indians, and in particular, their religions. I am interested in the image of the
noble red man as it continues to manifest itself particularly in
Europe, and I maintain that part of the reason the Indian continues to have high esteem in Europe is not solely because of
the works of Karl May and the general romantic interpretation
of the American Indian by European popularists and scholars, but because the American Indian who travels to Europe is
comfortable with the image. As I state in the essay, this point

of view might be considered heresy in some American Indian camps, but I have discussed the matter fully with American Indians in the United States who concur with my analysis. Whether romantic or not, the American Indian continues to make an impression on European populations some of whom support many of the political positions of contemporary Native American activists.[12]

The endnotes identify most of those people who have helped me formulate my thoughts about the topics under investigation here. By way of special emphasis I would like to thank all of the people at Pine Ridge for their continued support, particularly Zona Fills the Pipe, Clarence and Sadie Janis, Pugh and Etta Youngman, Bill and Nancy Horncloud, and Tom and Darlene Shortbull. Among my academic colleagues, I would like to thank Robin Fox and Solomon H. Katz particularly in relation to certain problems in biosocial anthropology. Of course I take full responsibility for my conclusions. Brother C. M. Simon, S.J., at the Heritage Center, Holy Rosary Mission, Pine Ridge, South Dakota provided a summer retreat of sorts and stimulating conversation. Janet Bascom provided badly needed editorial assistance. Nancy O. Lurie was kind enough to provide a critical assessment of the chapters, and I frequently followed her sage advice.

As usual, my wife, Marla N. Powers, was with me in the field and at home when all the essays were first written and gave me generously of an endless supply of insights and affection.

WILLIAM K. POWERS

Pine Ridge, South Dakota

BEYOND THE VISION

INTRODUCTION

LAKOTA whom I have known at Pine Ridge for the past forty years have said that the vision quest and the sweat lodge are the two oldest rituals. Although both are regarded as part of the seven sacred ceremonies of the Lakota, all brought simultaneously to the people by the White Buffalo Calf Woman, they are, to the great chagrin of scholars who expect religion to be rational, at once the predecessors of the seven rites and at the same time integral to them.[1]

Although the sweat lodge and other ceremonies have limitless sacred qualities, the vision quest differs from all of them in one important way. It is the most uniquely holy of all the religious ordeals because it constitutes a ritual encounter between an individual and the supernatural beings and powers he beseeches for whatever personal reasons. Unlike other rituals, it is not performed collectively. The supplicant, once he has vowed to be put on the hill by a medicine man, is on his own to face the challenges and possible dangers of the vigil. Alone at the top of a pine-covered hill such as those that proliferate on the Pine Ridge Reservation, or even standing at the summit of Bear Butte in the Black Hills near Sturgis, South Dakota, he waits for an appointed number of days and nights—as many as four—without the confidence and assurance inspired by fellow participants. Perhaps this is really why the vision quest is regarded as such a dangerous and frightening undertaking. Unlike the camaraderie, albeit a serious kind, found in the sweat lodge and other rituals, such as the Sun Dance, all that surrounds the supplicant on the hill are a string of minute tobacco pouches and colorful cloth offerings dedicated to the various spiritual helpers to whom he smokes the sacred pipe and prays. Whereas in these other ceremonies men and women may pray, sing, and dance together in a harmonious appeal to Wakantanka and the other important members of the Lakota pantheon, on top of the hill, the supplicant stands alone.[2]

The spirits he beckons are often capricious sorts. They are quite capable, during the intense seriousness of it all, of fooling him, playing pranks on him, deceiving him. Some of the more malevolent who occasionally enter the sacred place to cavort and interfere with his devoted intentions are capable even of harming him. But if he survives, if he "pulls through" as they say on the reservation, he will be given a special reward for his vigilance from the spirits. Most of all he will pray for a long life for himself and his relatives, and he will offer himself as a sacrifice so that these lives may be led together. And his prayers will be answered, so it is believed, as long as the supplicant understands all the mystical commands and mandates from the supernaturals that have communed with him. The process will not be easy, and never straightforward. These supernaturals will appear to him in the form of humans, sometimes tantalizing young women who will try hard to tempt and confuse him. Others will come as animals, birds, and reptiles; others will be mere insects, such as butterflies and dragonflies, ants, and of course, the mischievous Inktomi. Some of these visitors will taunt and threaten him, some will ridicule him, and some will frighten him because, after all, the vision quest is an ordeal whose ends are partly dependent on its means. The more difficult the endeavor, the greater the potential reward. If a long and healthy life with one's relatives is one's request, then no price is too high to pay for the individual dedicated to seeking knowledge in this traditional Lakota manner.

And if he believes in the power of the pipe, which according to the Lakota has enlightened people since the White Buffalo Calf Woman first carried it through a mist of ignorance, then he will overcome the dangers of the vision quest, he will live in peace with his neighbors, and with the help of a medicine man, make plans for his future. These plans will focus on his own personal goals and future success. If he is single, his incentive may be to understand what kind of an education he will require, or whether he should stay on the reservation or leave it. If he is married, the vision may suggest more pragmatic pathways to learn a trade, find a job, and eventually help raise a family. He will frequently seek guidance about personal difficulties—drinking, drugs, divorce, recalcitrant children, or simply a plethora of simple problems that has for the moment enveloped him.

Sometimes the vision may be in the form of an instruction intimating to the supplicant that he should walk with the pipe; that is, become a medicine man himself. No matter what the nature of the decision is, however, it must ultimately be interpreted by a wise man who has been on the quest himself and who derives his ability to interpret visions for others from an ongoing familiarity with his own spirit helpers. And the future success of the supplicant is obtainable and real only to the extent that he is able to follow the instructions and mandates from the supernaturals as perfectly and precisely as the interpretations of his mentor allow. A vision then is not only a blueprint for the future, but a theory about how one should live with himself and his relations and all the other creatures of the natural and cultural world.

If the supplicant is faithful in following the sometimes vagarious mandates from his spirit advisers, then he will, according to the belief system, be granted his wishes. But if he is careless and, as the Lakota say, stumbles with the pipe, great hardships will await him at the bottom of the hill. If it is felt that the instructions of the vision are unclear and have in fact caused difficulty and privation, and the medicine man himself is helpless to make further predictions, then it may be necessary for the moment to abandon the incomprehensible mysteries of the first vision and embark upon another. Perhaps a new vision will help clarify all that has been heretofore vague and unsettling.

Living up to the instructions and mandates of a vision, then, is much like testing a theory, and, like other theories

that are (for whatever reason) useful in explaining the phenomenon at hand, these may be discarded and replaced with
new theories and new visions, each subsequent one being
partly contingent on and inspired by the lack of clarity or inutility of the previous one. What is really important is the application of the vision to real life and the manner in which the
vision can accurately predict the potentiality of the supplicant, much as a theory predicts the nature of the subject
under examination. In the long run, after a series of trials and
errors, what really is important is that which lies beyond the
vision.

CHAPTER 1

THE VOCABLE: AN EVOLUTIONARY PERSPECTIVE

Most of [Flathead] music is without words, excepting upon
some special occasions they use *hi, ah,* in constant repetition, as we use fa, sol, la.
　　　　—Samuel Parker (1842; quoted in Merriam 1967, 34)

Ultimately we shall perhaps discover that the interrelation-
ship between nature and culture does not favor culture to
the extent of being hierarchically superimposed on nature
and irreducible to it. Rather it takes the form of a synthetic
duplication of mechanisms already in existence but which
the animal kingdom shows only in disjointed form and dis-
persed variously among its members—a duplication, moreover, permitted by the emergence of certain cerebral structures which themselves belong to nature.
　　　　—Lévi-Strauss (1969a, xxx; original 1949)

PERHAPS it is the fate of modern scholarship, as well as the
history of intellectual development, that those persons who
have originated some of the most significant ideas about human nature often lack a mechanism whereby their theories
may be implemented. Conversely, there are others—thinkers,
who are perhaps better labeled mechanics—who have discovered a method of implementing an idea but are not quite sure
just to what theory they would like to assign their method—
if, in fact, they want to assign it at all.[1]

　A case in point of the former is Darwin, who in the mid-
nineteenth century gave the world his theories of natural and
sexual selection, theories about how all organisms evolved in
relation to the degree that they could survive to successfully
reproduce newer generations, somehow better fitted to their
environment, an idea labelled later by Herbert Spencer as

"survival of the fittest," an expression often attributed to Darwin but never uttered by him. But Darwin, in his own time, never was able to identify the process of evolution—the mechanics if you will. It required the monk Mendel to suggest independently the mechanics of heritability without giving much consideration—in the quietude of his pea garden—to evolution itself. It was not until 1900 that the biologist, Hugo DeVries, took on the task of synthesizing Darwin's great idea with Mendel's mechanism to formulate what is regarded as the general theory of evolution; that is, evolution based on the principles of genetics.

It is also perhaps the fate of modern scholarship that although we are overwhelmed by the burgeoning methodologies and mechanics at our disposal, most of our mechanics are applied to the ideas of our antecedents; new ideas seem to be at a premium if, in fact, they exist at all.

It is in the spirit of synthesis that this chapter is offered. It begins with Samuel Parker's observation that there is something analogous between *hi*'s and *ah*'s and fa, sol, la's; it ends with Lévi-Strauss's suggestion that culture is somehow a duplication of structures already present in nature, a statement that links him irrefutably with Darwin, and in so doing suggests a dialectic based on biogenetic structuralism.[2] The major theory under consideration here is the evolution of music; the major mechanism, upon which this paper focuses, is a peculiar form of human sound occurring in both speech and song which, as I shall point out, functions among all human societies even though traditionally it has been associated with "primitive" music.

Despite the ubiquity of the linguomusical utterance known variously as vocable, burden syllable, meaningless syllable, and nonsense syllable, there is no current body of musicological, ethnomusicological, or anthropological theory that addresses itself to explaining the significance of this important medium of panhuman expression—structurally, functionally, or evolutionarily.[3]

The vocable, as I prefer to call it for reasons stated below, has not received the same descriptive and analytic attention as have other aspects of music, perhaps because of the fact that it lies somewhere between lexically meaningful speech, and musical expression devoid of a semantic range. The same anatomical and acoustical properties that govern speech also govern the vocabalic utterance, yet the latter is frequently sung in such a manner that it is stripped of nouns and verbs, subjects and predicates and thus of understanding. If, as Langer has stated, music has no "assigned connotation" (Langer, 1942:240), vocables, as an integral part of music, seem to be endowed at the onset with a double burden of explanation.[4]

Where the vocable has received moderate attention is in its association with drums, rattles, pulsating rhythms, pentatonic scales, absence of harmony, renditions of incomplete types, vocal tension, and other musical relationships raised to ontological status by means of the academic ritual of primitivization. Implicitly or explicitly ethnomusicologists, with little exception, agree with the philosophers that "our counterpoints and harmonic involutions have nothing like the expressive abandon of the Indian 'ky-yi' and 'how-how'" (Langer, 1942, 216). We are often cautioned that it is a mistake to reduce music to its origins and elevate primitive emotions to the "dignity of music" (Langer, p. 219). We may agree with the same philosopher, however, that probably song of some kind "is older than any musical interest" (Langer, p. 246).

The classicist C. M. Bowra perhaps sums up best the prevailing status of the vocable: "Song begins with some sort of tune and to adapt *real words* to it is a separate and subsequent task which calls for considerable dexterity" (Bowra 1962, 63; italics added). For Bowra, vocables belong in primitive song; they are the beginnings of man's proclivity to make music. But despite his ethnocentrism, Bowra is instructive in his evolutionary implications.[5]

Given the usual cultural bias with which they are discussed, it is not surprising that, in our recent interest in music universals, vocables are ignored. Yet, as Wachsmann has suggested, universals can be examined only if the word "music" is left out. He provides a tetradic schema in which universals should be investigated with respect to the (1) physical properties of

the sounds, (2) physiological response to acoustical stimuli,
(3) perception of sounds selected by the human mind based
on previous experience, and (4) the response to the environmental pressures of the moment (Wachsmann 1971, 382).

If Wachsmann had added another category to his schema,
one that investigates the relationships between his original
four categories and sounds produced by species other than
Homo sapiens, he may have had to answer the charges of
paternity-certainty when the newly emerging field of neuro-
musicology—or perhaps we should say sociobiomusicology—
came to seek a founding father, since Wachsmann anticipated
E. O. Wilson by four years.[6]

If we can for the moment ignore music and speak of the vocable as a kind of sound, then we may ask whether there is a
society in the world that does not somehow convey and enjoy
melodic and rhythmic stimulation through the utterances of
lexically meaningless acoustical properties.

It is to this end—that a systematic investigation of the structure and function of the vocable may serve to aid in understanding both general and specific relationships between
sound and culture—that this chapter is offered.[7] It is divided
into three parts, each of which focuses on a separate but related theme.

The first theme is that of structure, and I provide a rudimentary linguistic analysis of vocables employed in the singing of Plains Indian songs. From the perspectives of vocable, I
have the distinct advantage of being able to agree with both
Feld and Nattiez on the importance of linguistic analysis in
ethnomusicology.[8]

The second theme discusses the function of the vocable.
Here I hope to introduce several types of functions and suggest that in addition to the explanation by Fletcher (1900, 125)
that "many Indian songs have no words at all, vocables only
being used to float the voice"—a lyrical idea—vocables, in
fact, serve other communicative functions of both signal and
symbolic import.[9]

The third theme discusses the relationship of vocables to
the human mind and environmental pressures, and thus the

relationship of vocables to the origin and evolution of Homo
sapiens. I suggest the neural organization of sound that sub-
sequentially leads to the culturally relevant product of sound,
one that we label music, is a precondition of human cultural
evolution rather than a result of it.

I have selected the term vocable as the unit of analysis, or
rather the classification under which these units of sound may
be subsumed, in opposition to other labels that have the same
intended "meaningless" meaning: e.g., meaningless syllable,
burden syllable, nonsense syllable, fill-in syllable, meaningless vocable, and non-sense vocable, all of which appear ar-
bitrarily in the ethnomusicological literature.[10] There are two
important reasons why I choose *vocable*. The first is that it is at
once historical and commemorative: the first generation of
comparative musicologists, Densmore, Fletcher, and Curtis,
all used the term and agreed on its significance without offering any explanation for its prevalence. The second reason is
that all other terms are either value-laden or explicable only
by tautological means: a meaningless syllable has no meaning,
a nonsense syllable makes no sense, and so on.

Webster is not particularly useful; he defines vocable as a
word composed of various sounds or letters without regard to
its meaning. Provisionally, I define vocable as a unit of human
sound employed to transmit melodic and rhythmic information. After more research, the term "human" may have to be
eliminated, and perhaps the terms "conspecific and inter-
specific" added. I have purposely avoided the terms "word,"
"meaning," and "music(al)," and suggest that the distinction
between human and nonhuman sound, or word and meaning, from the perspective of vocable, can be understood only
on the basis of the context in which it is investigated; that is,
vocables have no intrinsic verbal or musical qualities outside
the context in which they function.

This latter point helps partly solve the problem which has
received attention, viz., Which came first: the vocable or the
word? or whether vocables are formed from archaic or dysfunctional words, or give rise to them, as many have argued.
Because ethnographic data so far point to historical explana-

tions for the occurrences of words giving rise to vocables and the reverse, there is no reason to assume that the primacy of one over the other is of any consequence except in a rather narrow historical context. The historical context is, of course, important for understanding, say, the process of diffusion and classification; but as an exclusive explanation it fails to lead us to generate nomothetic theories, and supports the belabored and unfounded thesis that the vocable is only a "primitive" expression of music.

STRUCTURE

On the basis of empirical data collected from a number of Plains Indian tribes,[11] I am led to the conclusion that in the populations studied there is an integral relationship between the distinctive features of the native language and the distinctive features that characterize each tribal inventory of vocables. The relationship between language and vocables, of course, is not new; my point here that any investigation of the vocable must begin precisely where linguistic research begins, i.e., with phonological considerations, rather than at the level of the morpheme or lexeme.

Structural linguistic method begins with the proposition that every language is constituted from a finite number of phonemes, minimal units of sounds, which combine to form morphemes, minimal units of meaning, and lexemes or lexemic sets, comparable to the word, according to rules. Knowledge of the rules enables one to generate an infinite number of meaningful utterances—language. Applying this theory to vocables, I seek to identify the finite set of phonemes that constitute each vocable. I conclude that a tribal inventory of vocables, however, unlike language, is itself finite.

On the basis of research among various Plains tribes, I have been able to construct models of tribal vocabalic sounds that are based on phonological rules. I will present five such models, called (1) Prototype, (2), Lakota, (3) Dakota, (4) Þegiha, and (5) Caddoan. Three tribal models represent members of the Siouan linguistic family and another, Cad-

Phonemes	Vocables	Cadence

```
  a e i o        a    e    i    o
h         ?      a?   e?   i?   o?
w                ha   he   hi   ho
y                ha?  he?  hi?  ho?        | we yo he ye he ye yo |
                 wa   we   wi   wo
                 wa?  we?  we?  wo?
                 ya   ye   yi   yo
                 ya?  ye?  yi?  yo?
```

Fig. 1. Prototype

doan. Although these models are incapable of generating other models that explain vocables in other culture areas, I am suggesting that it is possible to construct similar models for all tribal musics, and it is only after such constructions have been completed that cross-cultural comparison of American Indian vocables can begin. Following Hymes (1962), we must begin with an ethnography of sound.

Here I would like to inject a proposition: if there is an integral relationship between language and vocables, beginning with the sound of language and the respective sound of vocables contained within tribal inventories, and if it is possible to construct a linguistic map based on genetic and historical relationships among languages, then it seems plausible to construct such a map—a vocabalic map—for any geocultural area about which we have similar information.

Because there are perhaps three hundred or more tribal musical traditions in the United States and Canada (to be arbitrary), obviously the examples provided here are modest contributions to such a map. Nevertheless, I hope that the few examples serve the purpose of initially understanding the relationship between the sound of language and the sound of vocables as a future contribution to theory.

In fig. 1, Prototype, the consonants in the left-hand vertical column, the vowels in the horizontal row, and the single glottal stop in the last vertical column are all phonemes. Reading

Phonemes	Vocables	Cadence

a e i o u		Same as Fig. 1			
h	?	plus			
w	n	an in un			we lo he ye he ye yo
y		la le li lo			ye lo he ye he ye yo
l		la? le? li? lo?			

Fig. 2. Lakota

from left to right, consonants combine with vowels and glottal stops to generate the vocables in the second column marked vocables. The Prototype model accounts for those songs sung with vocables only. As we can see, eight phonemes generate 32 vocables. In the third column is an example of a cadential formula associated with the popular War Dance of the Northern and Southern Plains, generated from the combination of vocables.

In fig. 2, Lakota, named after the language spoken by seven western "Sioux" tribes, we see that we have added one consonant (*l*), one vowel (*u*), and a nasal marker (*n*), the latter of which when affixed to a vowel renders the vowel nasal. Note under Vocables that it is suffixed to only *an, in, un*.[12] This model generates the same number of vocables found in figure 1 but adds more: 11 phonemes generate 43 vocables. Unlike the Prototype, the Lakota and subsequent models account for all vocables employed in both songs using vocables only and those using both vocables and words.

Note in the Cadence column, however, that there are two variations of the standard War Dance cadence, the difference between the two being the initial phoneme of the initial vocable (*w* and *y*) and the substitution of *l* for *y* in the Prototype.

Figure 3, Dakota, named after the language of four eastern Sioux tribes is similar to Figure 2 with only one important exception: *d* is substituted for *l* and this substitution is reflected in the two variations of the cadence. Again 11 phonemes generate 43 vocables.[14]

Phonemes	Vocables	Cadence

a e i o u   Same as Fig. 1

h   ?   plus

| w   n | an   in   un | we do he ye he ye yo |
| y | da   de   di   do | ye do he ye he ye yo |

d   da? de? di? do?

Fig. 3. Dakota

Figure 4, Ɖegiha, is named after a Siouan subfamily composed of the Ponca, Omaha, Osage, Kansa, and Quapaw. It is similar to Figures 2 and 3 except that the substitutable consonant in the lefthand column is ɖ and this is reflected in the Cadence. Additionally, we find another nasal vowel (on): 11 phonemes generate 44 vocables.[15]

Finally, fig. 5, a generalized Caddoan model applicable to the Caddo and Wichita Indians of Oklahoma and named after the Caddoan linguistic family, adds both a "d" and an "n," and all five vowels are capable of nasalization, but this is not reflected in the single variation of the cadence. Twelve phonemes generate 53 vocables.

I would like to make some general remarks about the nature of the models presented here and their concomitant vocables and cadences:

1. The models have been drawn from ethnographic data, not the other way around. Yet the models may serve to generate hypotheses about vocabalic structure among musics of other societies.

2. I have provided examples of cadential formulas to show the subtle differences between tribal inventories of vocables, but the same rules that apply to the order in which vocables appear in the cadences also apply to the order in which they appear in other parts of the song structure, e.g., the theme. This leads to the formulation of some rules governing the examples:

Phonemes	*Vocables*	*Cadence*

a e i o u   Same as Fig. 1
h   ?   plus
w   n   an   in   on   un
y
ḓ   ḓa ḓe ḓi do
                  ḓa? ḓe? ḓi? ḓo?

we do he ye he ye yo
ye do he ye he ye yo

Fig. 4. Ɵegiha

a. The distinctive features of the vocable are homologous to the distinctive features of the singers' language. Therefore, phonological rules governing one govern the other.
b. Songs containing vocables only are likely to contain fewer vocables than those containing a combination of vocables and meaningful texts.
c. All vocables end with a vowel, either pure, nasal, or glottalized.
d. Pure and nasal a, e, and i are always followed by y plus vowel unless it is the final vocable in a song.
e. Pure and nasal o and u are always followed by w plus vowel unless it is the final vocable in a song.
f. Vowels ending in glottal stops may be reduplicated.
g. Only the consonant y may be substituted for another consonant.
h. Vocables found in a tribal repertory that are inconsistent with the above rules may be regarded as exotic or idiosyncratic.

Of course, a great deal more can be said about the structure of the vocable, but the major point I want to make is that rules govern both the selection and combinations of the vocables, and although they may or may not have lexical meaning (depending on the tribal inventory) they may be said to be "grammatical," and never arbitrary.[16]

Phonemes	Vocables	Cadence

a e i o u   Same as Fig. 1
h   ?   plus
w   n   an en in on un   we do he ye he ye yo
y   da de di do
d   da? de? di? do?
n

              na ne ni no
              na? ne? ni? no?

Fig. 5. Caddoan

FUNCTION

Ethnomusicologists generally agree that the primary—if not only—function of the vocable is that of serving as a medium of melodic expression. But given that vocables are governed by rules, and thus exhibit structural integrity and inflexibility, a number of equally important functions emerge. Generally, I divide these functions into two types, the signal and the symbolic, each of which contains four subtypes.

By signal function, following the linguist deSaussure,[17] I mean one in which there is a nonarbitrary relationship between the musical concept (what deSaussure called the signified) and the vocabalic unit(s) employed to convey that concept (deSaussure's signifier). The concept and its expression are always unambiguously related. To illustrate, let us examine the Western notion of Key. If the paradigm under investigation is the key of C, then the musical concepts to be expressed are C, D, E, F, G, A, B, the structural components of the paradigm. If we render in singing the key of C paradigm, that is, produce it syntagmatically (one note after the other), we employ the vocables do, re, mi, fa, sol, la, ti. Given that the paradigm is C, then there is a nonarbitrary relationship between C and do, D and re, E and mi, etc. This is to say that the vocables perform a signal function, of which there are several types: key of B♭, key of D, key of E♭, etc.

By symbolic function, I mean one in which there is an arbitrary relationship between the musical concept and the vocables employed to express it. Again in the Key of C paradigm, if I compose a piece of music for the first time, the relationship between the notes or vocables is arbitrary. Although I am bound by the non-arbitrary relationship between idea and expression paradigmatically, the syntagmatic relationships are purely arbitrary, and thus symbolic. The distinction between some signal functions and symbolic functions often requires context; e.g., once the piece has been composed, the symbolic relationships between musical concept and expression become signal, only again to exhibit symbolic relationships when the same piece of music is stylized or interpreted—that is, deviates unpredictably from the nonarbitrary relationships that led to its composition.[18]

The subtypes of these functions serve to explain a number of ways in which vocables are employed in American Indian societies, but it is likely that they may also explain vocabalic function universally. There are:

I. Signal Functions

A. Melodic Function. The vocable functions to convey melodic information, The melodic function is signal because, although there is no absolute relationship between tone and vocable, once composed, each tone is assigned a vocable, and the relationship remains fixed for the lifetime of the song. Any alteration of the vocable causes the song to be regarded as either new or different from the original, even when the melody itself remains unchanged. At one stage, that of composition, the relationship between melody and vocable is arbitrary; once the composition process is complete, the relationship becomes nonarbitrary.

B. Rhythmic Function. On those occasions when songs are sung without instrumental accompaniment, the vocable is frequently employed to convey rhythmic information among singers, as well as between singers and dancers. For example, vocal accents serve to identify "down beats" and thus are signal in that they represent nonarbitrary relationships between vocable and rhythmic information distinct from melodic information.

C. Generic Function. Because of the nonarbitrary relationship between vocables and melodic and rhythmic information, introductory phrases, mediating, and final cadences as well as subcadences serve to identify both the class of songs and the specific member of the class (cf. List, 1968). The cadences appearing in the figures above are examples of the generic function.

D. Cueing Function. Vocabalic phrases are capable of conveying information among singers, and between singers and dancers with respect to the number of times a song and dance may be repeated, and at what precise time it will end. In the examples of cadences in the figures, while they do not change rhythmically or melodically each time they are sung, they do change vocabalically; i.e., the final vocable varies between mediating cadences, and final cadences.

II. Symbolic Functions

A. Poetic Function. By poetic function I mean specifically the relationship between the vocable and song texts. Because, as stated above, vocables require some verbal or musical context in order to exist, the poetic function is symbolic because the vocable exists only in the context of the work, which is itself symbolic. Vocables may be employed in significant "grammatical" ways in order to render the text appropriate to the melody. For example, vocables may be prefixed, infixed, or suffixed to words and phrases. Here I offer a Lakota example: the words *oyate k'un*, which begin the phrase, "when the people gather." As an example of vocabalic prefix, we hear *he* oyate k'un; as infix, oyate *ye* k'un; as suffix, oyate k'un *yun*. Infixes and suffixes have a strong tendency to rhyme with the preceding syllable, and the rules influencing the ordering of phonemes in either language or vocables also hold when both words and vocables are combined.[19]

B. Mimetic Function. Vocables often serve as stylized versions of bird and animal cries, and these are often regarded as integral to the performance of the song, although not necessarily to its structure. In the mimetic function, the vocable is arbitrary and thus symbolic on two counts—from the perspective of its arbitrary position in the performance and from its ability to "stand for" an animal or bird.

C. Ornamentative Function. Individuals upon occasion render idiosyncratic versions of vocables that may be regarded as personal ornamentation. Important here is that often the melodic and rhythmic information remains constant, and the ornamentation is achieved exclusively through the manifestation of the vocabalic unit(s). Vocables used in this way are usually inconsistent with other vocables; e.g., among the Lakota, the vocable *c'e* was used as a personal signature by only one person.

The special manipulation of vocables may also function to serve as song group signatures or underscore a particularly desirable style. For example, Northern Plains singing is characterized by two types of introductory vocabalic renditions sung to the same melodic and rhythmic line. One introduction is called *pan* 'whining, crying' in Lakota/Dakota, and the other is *akiš'a* 'yelping.' The first is a sustained tone; the second, staccato. Since songs are usually composed with the staccato introduction, one employing perhaps eight to ten vocables, when the same vocables are sung in the sustained style, it is rendered as if it were simply holding one extended vocable. In order to keep the song group together, singers "think" the staccato vocables to themselves while they sing the sustained vocables.

D. Mnemonic Function. Vocables serve to elicit songs from memory when the melody has been temporarily forgotten. The vocabalic phrase may be hummed, whispered, whistled, or simply thought until its corresponding melodic and rhythmic information is called forth to consciousness. I regard this process as a symbolic function because frequently the mnemonic function will elicit a song other than the one intended, although usually one from the same genre.

So far, I have suggested that it is possible to investigate the vocable profitably with respect to its structure and function, demonstrating that vocables do not appear at random in the context of the song (nor could they unless the "music" was sung by an individual, and then perhaps he would be accused of singing gibberish if, in fact, he was accused of singing at all). I also demonstrated that vocables are capable of performing a number of functions aside from serving as a medium of melodic expression, and that these functions all have meaning although not in a semantic sense. To this end, the study of music, song texts, and vocables, along with other social and cultural institutions, rightly belongs to the field of semiotics.

The final point I would like to make here is in the form of a question: To what extent may the vocable, defined as a human sound functioning to convey melodic and rhythmic information, be a universal feature of humanity? If it can be demonstrated that all peoples have some preference for singing "meaningless syllables," then it should be of some interest to science why this should be so.

Although the examples employed here apply specifically to American Indians in a limited geographic area, it would be counterintuitive to assume that they do not appear in other parts of North America, or the Western hemisphere, or any other part of the world where ethnographers have reported on the "rude" peoples of the world. But what about contemporary music: art music of the East and West, church music, rock and roll, jazz, blues, country, western—or whatever genre is under consideration? Do not these musical traditions and genres also transmit melodic and rhythmic information by means of vocables?

Civilized music gives us do, re, mi, fa, sol, la, ti, do and the vocables employed to sing Indian ragas. Johnny could sing only one note—and it was the vocable *a:*. Scat singing in jazz music is entirely vocabalic. And the fifties produced do wah do wah, and rock produced *ui:* and yea, yea, yea. Earlier, hudsut rawston on the riverat, and mairsiedoats and doeseatoats are perfect examples of "enigmatic" sound set to music. Falalalalalalalala. Popeye the Sailor ma-boop boop! The woo: in the Atcheson Topeka and Santa Fe, Use Ajax, boom boom. Aya yay yay yay-Cielito Lindo. Abadabdabadaba-monkey talk. Zipadee do dah-zipadeeday. Ragmop dudiyatahdiyahdah.

Boop boop didam dadam waddam choo. Or simply boop boop ee do. Bongo, bongo, bongo. Oolala, and La Vie en Rose. I do not believe that these are isolated examples of worldwide vocables, each consistent with the native languages of the singers, and each having a structure and function not unlike those discussed for a few Native American tribes.

As Samuel Parker said in 1842, the vocables of the Flathead Indians are the same, structurally and functionally, as our own fa, sol, la. And perhaps vocables can be understood only if they are regarded as one of the means, perhaps the most important, by which human beings universally make music. This statement takes us directly to the relevance of the systematic study of vocables in reconsidering the origin of music.

EVOLUTION

Any theory that purports to explain the origin and evolution of music must begin with similar research on the origins and evolution of speech. First, one major criticism of earlier theories of language and music origin is that there is a difference between origin and evolution. Origin can happen once or many times, as we know from the archaeological literature telling us that pottery and the firing kiln, the bow and arrow, and the throwing spear have been invented, that is, originated, numerous times and in various parts of the world at different times. *Origin* may happen with a big bang as in the case of our universe, or perhaps less obtrusively in the stillness of a murky swamp, as in the case of microbes or even man himself. But at some period in time and space we must conclude that there is a *final* origin of things, and it is at this point that we are concerned with what that origin does with itself—where does it go, how does it develop, and into ultimately what? It is only then that we can be concerned about the evolution of that to which the final origin gave rise.

Origins require explanation, couched either in rules of theology or in rules of probability. But once originated, things begin, and continue to evolve, and we suspect that they do so in a number of ways ranging from random to calculated change.

We also imagine that there are rules to be discovered about the nature of evolution, rules based on sometimes evolutionary fragments of the past.

In the past, the haste with which ethnomusicologists in particular have dismissed origin theories is, I think, due to the fact that often they confuse origin with evolution. This is perhaps particularly so in the case of arguments against Darwinian theory of evolution, a theory that also takes into consideration the origin and evolution of music. Darwin, of course; has been recently reinvented or, at least, reinvoked, in current anthropological and sociobiological theories attempting to describe the evolution of human behavior in such a way that culture, once the exclusive domain of *Homo sapiens,* is viewed as the medium through which man adapts biologically to his environment.[20]

Not only has there been no distinction between origin and evolution in the writings and critiques of ethnomusicologists, but there has been a tendency for ethnomusicologists to follow their anthropological forebears, particularly American and British anthropologists who suggest that culture is somehow reified and detached from biology, as if some imaginary bridge had separated the two. Metaphorically, many anthropologists have burned the bridge behind them so that biological evolution and cultural evolution drift apart. In the holocaust, Darwinian evolutionary theory, which relies on natural and sexual selection, is left back behind the blaze only to be rescued by biologically oriented anthropologists but hardly ever by ethnomusicologists.

Nettl, for one, in his survey of theories on the origin of music, exemplifies what may be viewed as the cultural bias. After reviewing the most popular theories: Darwin's sexual theory, i.e., music originated as a form of "mating calls"; Buechel's theory that music developed in work songs; Stumpf's theory that music originated in a need to communicate over long distances; and Nadel's theory that music originated as a special means of communicating with the supernatural, Nettl makes the important observation that those theories that have received the most universal acceptance are those linking music to language. He tells us that "the view that music originated from 'impassioned' speech was held by Jean Jacques Rousseau, Herbert Spencer, and Richard Wagner" (Nettl 1956, 135). He then offers his own theory which is "based on the assumption that an undifferentiated method of communication existed in remote times, one which was neither speech nor music but which possessed the three features which they hold in common: pitch, stress, and duration."

Nettl postulates "three stages in the *development* of music: (1) undifferentiated communication; (2) differentiation between language and music, with music still in a highly elementary stage; and (3) differentiation between various musical styles" (Nettl, 1956:136; italics added). This, of course, contrary to earlier statements, is not a theory about the origin of music. Rather, it is about the evolution (Nettl's "development") of music, one which presupposed that language somehow precedes music, or is at least in a higher form of development. But there is no reason, other than a cultural bias, which suggests that humans have some rudimentary form, or perhaps developed form of language before they can become human, that language must precede music. In fact, Nettl's first stage of undifferentiated communication might be conceived of as a stage in which the predecessors of both language and music exist and give rise to music and language or language and music, but in no particular order of importance.

If we distinguish between origin and evolution, then all of the theorists who have been summarily dismissed because of the illogicality of their positions can be reinvoked. Darwin suggests some idea of how music (and language) may have originated through some mechanism that enhanced sexual selection. The other theories, those by Buecher et al., essentially address the problem of differentiation among music styles. The above theories are not in conflict; each is of a separate order.

I would like to return to Darwin's view of the origin and evolution of music, or more rightly, song, the so-called sex-linked hypothesis (Greenway, 1976:10).

Darwin was certainly not the first to suggest that human

speech was somehow shaped by grunts and growls, some of which were perhaps set to music. In *The Descent of Man*, Darwin pays homage to Lord Monboddo and Dr. Blacklock, the latter quoted (in Monboddo 1774) as having stated that "the first language among men was music, and that before our ideas were expressed by articulate sounds, they were communicated by tones varied according to different degrees of gravity and acuteness" (Darwin 1871; Modern Library Edition, n.d., 880).

Darwin himself, in criticizing Herbert Spencer's theory, one also consonant with Diderot's, stated that cadences used in emotional speech gave rise to music. Darwin, of course, insisted that "musical notes and rhythm were first acquired by the male or female *progenitors* of mankind for sake of charming the opposite sex" (Darwin 1871, 880).

In his seminal work "The Origin and Function of Music," Spencer's general position is that "all feelings . . . pleasurable or painful, sensations or emotions—have this common characteristic, that they are muscular stimuli," and that there is "a direct connection between feeling and motion." He states:

> We have here . . . a principle underlying all vocal phenomena, including those of vocal music, and by consequence those of music in general. The muscles that move the chest, larynx, and vocal chords, contracting like other muscles in proportion to the intensity of the feelings . . . it follows that variations of voice are the physiological results of variations of feeling; it follows that each inflection or modulation is the natural outcome of some passing emotion or sensation. [Spencer 1857, 397–98]

All of this so far does not conflict with Darwin's assumption that the utterances of musical sounds "become associated with the strongest emotions of which [human beings] were capable—namely ardent love, rivalry and triumph" (Darwin, 1965:87). Darwin, in fact, in both this and an earlier work speaks of the power of music to recall,

> in a vague and indefinite manner, those strong emotions which were felt during long-past ages, when, as is probable, our early progenitors courted each other by the aid of vocal tones. And as

several of our strongest emotions—grief, great joy, love, and sympathy—lead to the free secretion of tears, it is not surprising that music should be apt to cause our eyes to become suffused with tears. [Darwin 1965, p. 217]

It is not, then, the relationship between song and emotion over which Darwin and Spencer disagree; it is only over the priority of song over speech, where Spencer maintains that "what we regard as the distinctive traits of song are simply the traits of emotional speech intensified and systematized" (Spencer, 1857:402). And where Darwin reasons that

as we have every reason to suppose that articulate speech is one of the latest, as it certainly is the highest, of the arts acquired by man, and as the instinctive power of producing musical notes and rhythms is developed low down in the animal series, it would be altogether opposed to the principle of evolution, if we were to admit that man's musical capacity has been developed from the tones used in impassioned speech. We must suppose that the rhythms and cadences of oratory are derived from previously developed musical powers. We can thus understand how it is that music, dancing, song, and poetry are such very ancient arts. We may go even further than this, and . . . believe that musical sounds afforded one of the bases for the development of language. [Darwin 1965]

Anthropologists and ethnomusicologists tend to maintain a stronger allegiance to Spencer than to Darwin, with the notable exception of most physical anthropologists, particularly those who favor sociobiological approaches to explaining human behavior.

Although sociobiology has not imprinted, so to speak, upon music at large, and an understanding of sociobiology is not critical to this chapter, I should like to abstract from Konrad Lorenz's preface to the most recent edition of Darwin's *The Expression of the Emotions in Man and Animals* (despite the cautious title *Man* and *Animals*) the work to which most physical anthropologists and behavioral biologists would refer as the *locus classicus* of their own mutual interest:

[The] fact . . . is quite simply that behavior patterns are just as conservatively and reliably characters of species as are the forms of bones, teeth, or any other bodily structures. Similarities in inherited behavior united the members of a species, or a genus, and even the largest taxonomic units in exactly the same way in which bodily characters do so. The conservative persistence of behavior patterns, even after they have outlived, in the evolution of a species, their original function, is exactly the same as that of organs; in other words, they can become "vestigial" or "rudimentary," just as the latter can. [Lorenz, in Darwin 1965, xii]

Applying this statement to music: Music is a behavior that has evolved over long periods of human evolution, as have the human nose, the appendix, and the opposable thumb. There is no reason to assume that primitive—that is, incipient—music should resemble contemporary music any more than it is reasonable to expect contemporary musicians to maintain anything but vestiges of a prognathous jaw or a supraorbital ridge.

Returning to Nettl's criticism of Darwin, Lorenz dismisses Darwin's "mating-call" theory on the basis that other primates have no "song." Nonhuman primates, however, are quite capable of differentiating between numerous types of calls. The Indri and gibbon noted by Buettner-Janusch (1966:336) have "wailing territorial songs." Marler tells us that gibbons have thirteen cries, while howler monkeys have fifteen to twenty (Marler 1973, 336). The obvious problem here is a semantic one, and any theory about the origin of music must carefully distinguish between music, song, call, and cry as types of differentially produced sound.

Buettner-Janusch does not explore the relationship between song and speech but does state with respect to language that "man's imitation of sounds he hears in his environment, including sounds heard from other animals, must be one of the roots of origin" and ponders why there should be any question about this point, "for it seems obvious that a vocal language *could arise only as a modification of existing vocal systems*" (Buettner-Janusch 1966, 336; italics added). This does not place a particular emphasis on the position of, say, onomatopoeia in the origin of language, only on the capacity for protohumans to initiate it. Onomatopoeia, of course, figures prominently in the evolution of music and language. Buettner-Janusch suggests that "mimicking may have developed from the ability to answer a call with an imitation of the call itself," which apparently is possible even among lemurs (*Lemur catta*) if "only in a crude way" (Buettner-Janusch, p. 339).

Livingstone, in asking the provocative question, "Did the australopithicines sing?" (Livingstone 1973, 25–29), suggests that lower and middle Pleistocene hunters had a great territorial range, and vocal calls of different pitch might help establish territoriality, "territorial songs" thus leading hominids to preadapt to language.

Of course, the problem here again is terminological. There is no reason to assume that *Homo sapiens* invented or even developed music or song to communicate over long distances, inasmuch as other primates communicate over similar distances by uttering cries and calls. Stated another way, if one species' call is another's song, then the problem is not so much in the structure and function of sound units as it is in prescribing the appropriate form for labeling such sound differentiation.

Insofar as music, song, or for that matter, cries and calls leave no impression in the archaeological record, we may only logically deduce how differentiated sound became structured in such a way that a closed system of sound became an open one. Hockett and Ascher (1964), in a critical paper, address themselves to this problem and proffer a logical manner in which a half-dozen or so distinct signals, each of which was a response to a recurrent and biologically important event to protohominids, evolved into such an open system of symbols. This evolution from closed to open system occurs, according to the authors, when protohominids find a need to blend calls that normally are mutually exclusive. For example, the discrete sound that signaled food might be added to or blended with one signaling imminent danger, thus becoming in the process of transformation, food-danger. Over time, such a combination of sound differentiations would become part of the standard "vocabulary," given that there was survival value in the neologism. Formally stated, their theory appears as such:

Let ABCD represent the acoustical properties that would cause protohominids to focus their attention on the situation "food here." Let EFGH represent the acoustical properties associated with the situation "danger coming." In still another situation, finding both food and danger, the two acoustical sets would conflate to form ABGH. As this set becomes standardized, the acoustical set may be said to contain the components AB = food; CD = no danger; EF = no food; GH = danger. Logically, these components are capable of recombining to produce EFCD = no food, no danger.

Count (1964), in a critical response to the Hockett and Ascher paper, argues that brain mechanisms must operate *before* vocalization can be effected. He would look for processes of an organic nature to account for language, rather than a literal formula of permutations. As an alternative, Count suggests the coalescence of vocalic and mimetic responses as integral to the formation of speech, i.e., a blending of distance communications (calls) with proximate communications (mimetics), the latter of which predominate in gregarious animals. This critique is, of course, constant with Livingstone's "territorial song" but adds another dimension, mimetics, also suggested by Buettner-Janusch.

At this point I would like to return to the vocable and suggest some reasons why I consider it important from an evolutionary perspective. First, if the relationship between the origin of speech and the origin of song obtains, and all theories seem to support this relationship, and, second, if a priority is given to differentiated sounds that function in analogous or homologous ways across species for the purpose of signaling food, danger, sexual state, etc., then we must state that song, as Lenneberg (1964) has stated for speech, is built into man's brain. And although, like speech and language, song and music differ from one region or social group to the next, they do, of course, show some universal principles with respect to tempo, rhythm, pitch, timbre, and scale, not unlike those analogous features found in speech, even though sometimes in a less accentuated form.

In addition to these diagnostic features, the vocable also becomes a universal feature of song, and perhaps in some societies even instrumentation may be translated into a form of vocabalization, as it is, say, in jazz singing, where human voices imitate instrumental sounds, and instrumental sounds are often explained as imitative of human voices.

Now returning to evolutionary theory, it is axiomatic that those anatomical features or associated behaviors that survive in the species have or have had adaptive values; that is, they have enabled the human organism to adapt successfully to the environment. What I am suggesting here is not that vocables are somehow in themselves adaptive. Rather, I am suggesting that the process of structuring vocables is analogous to the process of structuring speech and song, and it is in this structuring process that we find a common denominator between speech and song.

This structuring process is, of course, in the domain of neuroanatomy and neurophysiology and has direct implications on the evolution of the human brain.[21] The structuring process is itself the manner in which the brain organizes experience; and as the brain evolves, so does the capacity to organize experience. We know from research that the brain evolves differentially with respect to structure and function, resulting in hemispheric specialization. Although the results of this research are still far from conclusive, there is a general agreement that the left hemisphere is largely responsible for making logicodeductive operations and generally, although not exclusively, controls speech and other analytic functions. The right hemisphere is largely, but again not exclusively, associated with synthetic, creative functions. The hemispheres are, of course, interoperative through the corpus callosum, and under some circumstances the functions of one hemisphere may be partly or fully assumed by the other.

I am intrigued by how utterances that are structured but have no semantic meaning may have affected the coordination of hemispheres over evolutionary times. There are at least two discriminating functions that may have direct bearing on such vocabalic utterances. The first function deals with the manner in which some nonsensical utterances have the capacity to desensitize the functions of one hemisphere, producing a kind of mechanism for short-circuiting, if you will, one hemisphere of the brain so that function is shifted to the other.

In analyzing the relationship between structures of the brain and the phenomenon of ritual trance, Lex writes that

> in certain meditation techniques reduction of sensory inputs by means of repetition of a *mantram*, a mellifluous sound, has the effect of monopolizing the verbal-logical activities of the left hemisphere, leaving the right hemisphere to function freely. Conversely, response to the rhythms of chanting and singing, dancing, handclapping, and percussion instruments engages right-hemisphere capabilities, concomitantly evoking the "time-less" quality of the attendant experience. [Lex 1979, 126]

Although Lex qualifies her statement by adding that Hindu students state that mantra is a mystical sense, the point here is that a mantra is structurally and perhaps functionally analogous to a vocabalic utterance. Once agreed, then one has only to seek the kind of adaptive significance promoted by an utterance of this sort. Lex suggests that, as a working hypothesis, one might consider the effect on such rituals as maintaining a homeostasis between energy-expending and energy-conserving behavior "acquired from genetic inheritance and influenced by experience" (Lex 1979, 146). This process tends to promote a feeling of well-being and at the same time "tune" the central nervous system by lessening the inhibitions of the right hemisphere. Lessening the inhibitions of the right hemisphere renders operable more synthetic capabilities of the brain, including creative functions such as nonverbal aspects of music.[22]

Keeping this first function in mind, we can turn to a second related one, the relationship between the structuring process of the brain and memorization. It does not require neurobiological sophistication to understand the relationship between music and memory. One need only look at various educational techniques from teaching the ABC's (itself a perfect example of vocabalic music) to radio and television products that are presumably more salable when set to music than when strictly verbalized.

Over evolutionary time, then, from the instant the first protohominid was able to replicate the first sound of a fellow protohominid, any evolutionary means of guaranteeing that a discrete sound would be committed to memory must be considered adaptive. But as Buettner-Janusch has told us, any instance of these vocalizations could arise only as a modification of existing vocal system. Thus we must turn to Darwin's earliest suggestion that "rhythms and cadences of oratory are derived from previously developed musical powers" if we can agree that these "musical powers" are, in fact, primitive communication systems employed to discriminate between potential sexual partners—and the availability of food and all other signals (such as territorial calls and danger)—being derived from these essential two, as Hockett and Ascher suggest.

My belief that the very foundation of speech and song rests on these essential two categories recalls Darwin's major hypothesis and his detractors' major criticism, which is to say that speech evolved from song and, in humans, song evolved by already present communicatory signals employed essentially for the purpose of attracting potential mates. These ideas, of course, are associated with Darwin's theory of sexual selection that has been revived recently and has become a major position of sociobiologists such as Hamilton (1971), Trivers (1971, 1972), and Wilson (1975).

Darwin's theory is more specific than is usually discussed in musicological origins literature. For Darwin, sexual selection was in the purview of females, which explains why males of the species are the ones endowed not only with more spectacular visual adornment but with vocal ornamentation. The argument goes like this (after Daly and Wilson 1978, 56–79): Animals have limited resources to expend on reproduction, and females generally invest more in each offspring than do males, thus having lower reproductive success: Some sire more than a single female can bear, while others die barren. There is greater reproductive competition between males over the right to inseminate a female, the female's greater parental investment being the resource over which males compete. A male courts indiscriminately, but a female must be selective in choosing a reproductive partner, since mismating can cost her much wasted nurture and lost reproductive potential.

It is the males, then, who court the females, who compete for the right to copulate with her; and if she is smart, she will choose those mates who will invest themselves in helping her to parent the offspring, thus helping to ensure that the next generation will survive to reproduce again. From the perspective of song, then, a human vocal system is essentially one that serves as a courting call, one that enables a female to distinguish a member of the opposite sex, and of the same species. This is a very powerful explanation, not merely for vocabalic music but for music in general. It helps us answer the age-old question why even today males dominate the field of music and dance in all known societies of the world.

If we regard evolution as opportunistic in the sense that all modifications are based on existing structures, then the sine qua non of existing structures must be the same for protohominids as it is for other species: a communications system that serves primarily to identify members of the opposite sex, particularly at the physiologically proper state of sexual receptivity. Food and sex are the only two prerequisites that will guarantee the reproductive success of the species. Everything else, from an evolutionary point of view, is superfluous.

If these are the protostructures of human existence, then we need not be concerned with the proposition that speech emerged from man's musical powers. Rather, we should state that speech emerged from a preexistent communication system employed primarily for the purposes of establishing sexual unions and signalling the presence of food, as well as other concomitant signals such as danger and enemies.

Although the question of the origin and evolution of music has not seriously concerned ethnomusicologists for nearly two decades, it is important to consider that in more recent times the issue has raised its head outside ethnomusicological circles. A relevant book (Critchley and Henson 1977) has attempted to look at the neurology of music. In a review Judd has asked some pertinent questions:

> The survival value of language is so obvious that it is rarely questioned, and the selective pressures leading to the evolution of language capacity as a universal in the human species are not a subject of great debate, but this is not the case for music. The survival value of music is far from clear, and this leads to many questions: Did language evolve first to somewhere near its present state and music emerge at that point, building on the highly evolved language capacities as a stylized form of speech (cf. Spencer, 1857)? Or was it the other way around: Was there a complex 'musical' calling system which became differentiated into speech as Darwin (1871) suggested? More realistically, to what extent did language and music emerge and separate from an already evolved communications system? [Judd 1979, 390]

It seems we have come full circle. From a Darwinian point of view, however, these questions, challenging as they are, need not be asked. It is not so much the question: Which came first, speech or song? as much as it is the question: Would *Homo sapiens be* the species that it is without a precondition for song? This is to say that *Homo sapiens* is the species that it is *because* of the peculiar way in which primitive communications evolved.

In summary, any theory that attempts to explain the origin *and* evolution of music must take into consideration the following points:

1. Protohominids were endowed with a communication system based on differentiated sound capable of discriminating between experiences associated with successful reproduction of the species, i.e., nourishment of the organism, and state of sexual receptivity.

2. The development of the neocortex and the concomitant hemispheric specializations of the brain are the result of the pressures of natural and sexual selection.

3. Part of this development includes the neural organization of

experience in such a way that (a) homeostasis is maintained between the two hemispheres, the left hemisphere capable of making mainly analytic operations and the right hemisphere governing mainly synthetic operations; and (b) memorization is enhanced.

4. Since all evolutionary modifications of the organism, here *Homo sapiens,* are based on existing structures, both speech and song emerge from primitive structuring processes associated with differentiated sounds that focus on food and sexual state.

5. Since the left hemisphere is mainly associated with speech and the right hemisphere in this case is mainly associated with song, a structuring process that relied on diagnostic features such as melody, rhythm, pitch, timbre evolved as a means of fine tuning the central nervous system with respect to creating homeostasis between energy-expending and energy-conserving systems.

6. A structuring process with both the features of song and a form of vocalization that carries no semantic weight became a significant means of neural organization of experience.

7. The need to differentiate between male and female members of the species required that this structuring process be differentiated so that males could be identified by their particular vocalizations to attract females who would then select them for mating.

8. As larger groups of human populations became differentiated, there continued differentiation not only between males and females but also between social groups.

9. Those features of song that continue to have a stabilizing effect on the anatomy and physiology of the brain should not be considered as vestiges of human articulation. Rather they should be regarded as an ongoing structural process of the brain. Vocables, along with instrumentation, hand-clapping, humming, whistling, and other articulated forms of music should be regarded as the results of a long period of hominid evolution in which these features enable *Homo sapiens* to adapt successfully to his environment.

If there is to be a theory that explains the origin and evolution of song, then it must be powerful enough to explain the origin and evolution of all incipient human characteristics. A bioevolutionary theory is the only theory powerful enough to do so. If, however, the goal of musicology and ethnomusicology is simply to understand cross-cultural similarities and differences in the musics of the world, then the problem of origin and evolution obviously need not be considered. In either case, whatever man does as a human animal, as Fox[23] has so aptly pointed out, he does because the human characteristics that we call culture *is* man's biological adaptation to the environment, a means of survival selected from his long evolutionary past.

CHAPTER 2

REGULATING A WAR DANCE: NONVERBAL CUES AROUND AN OGLALA DRUM

THIS chapter is concerned with nonverbal cues that regulate the commencement, duration, and termination of a War Dance, a major event in the contemporary powwow.[1] An Oglala variant is examined for the purpose of demonstrating how singers and dancers interact to coordinate the singing and dancing, exclusive of semantic and vocabalic texts, which are part of the song structure.

Employing sociolinguistic approaches[2] to nonverbal behavior, I provide a typology based on oral-aural, and gestural-visual codes. It explains the range and variation of nonverbal cues that are employed by singers and dancers to simultaneously regulate an entire War Dance and evaluate its progress.

Although at one time, before the 1950s, war dances were regulated by means of a conventional number of song renditions,[3] recent trends from North Dakota and Canada have given rise to a new musical format in which an unrestricted number are sung as accompaniment to the war dance. Additionally, Oklahoma influences have affected the dance style, mandating in particular that dancers must stop dancing precisely on the last beat of the drum (and song).[4]

This chapter addresses a specific problem: How do singers and dancers know when to start and stop singing and dancing?

SOCIAL SETTING

On the Pine Ridge Reservation, the Oglala hold their powwows both indoors and outdoors, depending on the season.

The typical outdoor powwow on which I focus is held in a circular shade modeled after a Sun Dance arbor. The dance portion of the shade is approximately 150 feet in diameter; the Sun Dance pole, or, in secular shades, the flagpole, is in the center of the dance area. Extending 10 to 15 feet beyond the dance area around the entire perimeter of the shade (with the exception of an entrance at the east) is a shade constructed of pine trees. The spectators and groups of singers sit under this shade while the dancers perform in the open. During rest periods, the dancers usually retire to the shade and sit near the singers.

Close to the entrance is an elevated announcer's booth and a public address system. The announcer coordinates the powwow and officiates at giveaways and other ceremonies that form an integral part of the powwow. Beyond the shade, there are numerous food stands, craftwork displays, and administrative tents.

The powwow normally lasts for two or three days. Dances begin in the early afternoon and continue through midnight with a break for dinner.[5] The success of a powwow is at least partly determined by the number of song groups and dancers participating. A shade of the dimensions just described can accommodate 1,000 dancers, although 500 is closer to the average. Traditionally, participants come from miles away and pitch their tents beyond the dancer area. There is a tendency for the powwows to increase in momentum as the days progress, with most dancers appearing on the last day or two.

THE SINGERS

The Pine Ridge Reservation is divided into districts for administrative purposes. The districts are, in turn, divided into communities that comprise people whose antecedents were members of extended family hunting groups. Ideally, when there is a tribal powwow, each district or community is represented by a song group.[6]

The song group contains a leader and four or five men who

normally sing together. At celebrations, the nuclear group may be augmented by individuals who "sing around." The group leader is essentially an administrative leader but often is also the song leader on the basis of having a good voice and large repertory of songs.

The song groups are often named: The Red Cloud Singers, the Sioux Travellers, the Porcupine Singers, Red Leaf Singers, and so on—names usually derived from their communities or districts. The group leader is also a "manager" and negotiates on behalf of the group for singing jobs off the reservation. On the reservation, singers provide their services at no charge but are often compensated by means of giveaways. For tourist attractions, they receive "day money."[7]

The paraphernalia of the song group includes a drum, usually of the marching-band variety, and a portable public address system. Each singer supplies his own drumstick, a section of a fishing pole or arrow shaft that has a taped handle and soft head made from various types of real and synthetic fur. Singers also provide their own folding chairs.

By convention, groups of singers sit under the shade, around the drum, in a place that tradition has reserved for them.[8] At larger powwows, ten or fifteen drums may perform, but in theory, one group is adequate. The public address system is set up, and the microphone cord is draped over the pine boughs above and allowed to extend over the center of the drum. The quality of the public address systems varies, and those systems of poor quality make it impossible for songs to be heard by dancers on the opposite side of the dance shade. There is a tendency, then, depending on audibility, for the dancers to move toward the drum that is performing rather than distribute themselves evenly over the dance area.

Although singers are predominantly males, one or two female singers may also perform regularly with the group. During the course of the dance, females from other districts may join in with the group.

THE SONGS

War Dance song structures are standardized and form a genre of Oglala music. The performance of one complete song includes six components:

    1. The introduction, a segment sung by the song leader only, which sets the pitch of the song and identifies the theme.
    2. The "second," a reiteration of the introduction sung by another man or the entire chorus.
    3. The theme, sung by the group.
    4. The cadential formula, sung by the group.
    5. A reiteration of the theme, sung by the entire group.
    6. The final cadential formula, sung by all except the leader, who again begins the next rendition when more than one song is sung.[9]

The conventional way of singing War Dance songs before 1950 was to repeat the six components four times, adding a coda, or "tail," as a finale. A dancer could simply count the renditions or listen for the final cadential formula and know when the song was ending. After the North Dakota influence, however, it could never be determined by the same criteria when the song was going to end because the number of renditions was determined by different criteria.

THE DANCERS

Men, women, and children perform as individuals, not groups, in the War Dance. For men and boys, war dancing is weaving a number of standardized steps into freestyle combinations with particular emphasis on head movement, angular body style, and intricate footwork. The women's style is less spectacular and resembles simply walking in time to the drum and song. There has been a relatively recent trend for the male dancers to move clockwise around the pole, while the women stay toward the outer perimeter of the dance area, moving counterclockwise. There are a number of variations, however, and the North Dakota style has provided

Omaha or "War" Dance at Pine Ridge, South Dakota, September 14, 1945. Courtesy U.S. Department of the Interior Library.

more liberation for female dancers in individual style, generalized movement, and intricacy of foot and body movement.

At any single powwow, there will be a variation of style ranging from the slow, reserved "old-time" dancing to the modern "fancy" dancing.

Oglala protocol dictates that dancers must be costumed. Men and boys wear hair roach headdresses, matching neck and back bustles, elaborate beaded and fringed breechcloths, cuffs, belts, harnesses, chokers, and moccasins. Most adult male dancers wear bells around their knees or ankles and carry whistles either carved of wood or fashioned from pipe tubing. These whistles are blown at particular times during the War Dance and serve as one of the cues between the dancers and singers indicating that the dance should be extended.

Rabbit Dance at Rosebud, South Dakota. The singers are huddled around the drum in center of the dance arbor ca. 1940s. Women are dancing as partners. Courtesy Heritage Center, Inc., Holy Rosary Mission, Pine Ridge, South Dakota.

Women and girls wear buckskin or cloth dresses reminiscent of the mid-nineteenth century. During the course of a War Dance, women may dance up next to the performing drum and join in with the male singers. To attract a number of female singers is synonymous with positively evaluating the performance of the singers and the selection of the song.

COMMENCEMENT

The powwow begins before all the singers, dancers, and spectators arrive. The first group of singers usually begin to sing for their own enjoyment while the announcer coaxes other singers and dancers to the shade over the public address system. The singers are assigned numbers so that each group may sing in turn as the announcer calls out its number.

Finally, as more singers and dancers arrive, the powwow officially begins, often ceremonially with a flag song or honoring song. After the official opening, the singers begin.

The initial songs of a powwow require few if any nonverbal

cues. But as the singing and dancing progress, singers in particular may become fatigued. Just as the singers are waning, the dancers are becoming enthusiastic. It is at this point that the singers begin to switch off leads, often—but not always—allowing most if not all singers around the drum a chance to start the next rendition of a song. Often, too, the leader of the song may want to end it, but more enthusiastic singers around the drum want to extend it. In this case, we find a number of nonverbal cues coming into play to determine the course of the song, frequently with split-second judgments being made by the principals.

PERFORMANCE OF THE SONG

When a leader wishes to start a song, he may strike the drum once loudly and immediately begin the introduction. During subsequent renditions of the song, he may again strike the drum loudly, this time enunciating the striking motion by raising the drumstick higher than he normally does. Often, the leader of the subsequent rendition will begin striking the drum loudly in duple beats while the group sings the final cadential formula. He must somehow attract the attention of the rest of the group, particularly after four or five renditions, or they will not know that he wants them to continue the song.

When singers like the song, enthusiasm may be demonstrated either by crying out, "Yooooo!" or by waving a drumstick in the air in small circles. Should one of the group demonstrate this kind of enthusiasm, it is a clear indication that the song will be extended. If the leader is not fatigued, he will simply start the next rendition. If he is becoming tired, however, he may throw off or pass the lead to another singer, possibly the one showing the most enthusiasm. In this case, the leader looks directly at those singers who are looking at him and points with his chin in a gesture that asks, "Are you going to start it?" If a person designates "Yes," he does so by nodding his head affirmatively or by raising his drumstick in an exaggerated way as if to strike the drum. If a person does not want to start the song, he shrugs off the lead by shaking his head negatively or by pointing his drumstick at another singer whom he wishes to take the lead. The person to whom the stick is pointed thus indicates by the same gesture whether he accepts or declines the invitation. If no one accepts the lead and all are tired, the leader will wave his free hand over the drum, palm down, back and forth, indicating that the song will be ended on the next final cadence. He may also wave his drumstick over the surface of the drum as a similar cue to stop.

It should be noted that all the above nonverbal cues are being enacted while the singers are singing, drumming, and that the transactions take place in a matter of seconds—during that segment of the song in which the theme is being repeated. Additionally, although the texts and vocables of the song indicate the continuity of a song, they do not predict its overall length of the dance. No songs may end prematurely; that is, not until the final cadence is sung. An agreement on the final cadence is acknowledged by the dancers (when they do not hear the introduction) and thus the dancers may end their dancing precisely with the singers, being familiar with the structure of the final cadence.

During respites between War dances, singers may verbally discuss the specific songs they will sing for the next dance. They may practice them by singing softly or even listen to tape recorders for ideas. During the song, however, there are no verbal cues.

PERFORMANCE OF THE DANCE

When the song begins, eager dancers may immediately enter the shade and begin dancing. Most, however, wait for one complete rendition of the song to transpire before they begin.[10]

If the singers have an adequate public address system, dancers may perform anywhere within the confines of the dance area. They may begin dancing in a circle around the center pole or simply stay near their benches under the shade. If a song is particularly liked or if the public address system is inadequate, groups of dancers will slowly move toward the performing singers. Women who like to sing and who like the song will dance toward the singers until they are directly in front of the drum, facing the singers. There they continue to dance in place but join in with the singers during each rendition of the song at the beginning of each new theme. Women sing one octave above the men and can be heard well even without a public address system. For a number of women to dance up to the drum and begin singing is therefore a positive evaluation of the song and singers and will encourage the singers to extend the song and the dancers to continue dancing even more enthusiastically. As the momentum builds, both with more elaborate dancing and the tempo of the drum, dancers who wish to insure that the song is extended will dart up to the drum, as close as they can get, and blow their whistles over the heads of the singers. This is a command to the singers to extend the song; and if the singers are fatigued, increasing nonverbal cues are enacted around the drum between the singers as well as between the dancers and singers.

Female singers and dancers may upon occasion demonstrate their approval of the song by ululating.[11] The ululation may come during the course of the song or immediately after the dance has ended. If the latter is the case, the ululation suggests that the singers will begin the coda, or tail, but that it, too, like the main corpus of the song, will be extended. Like the whistle blowing, ululation is equally an encouragement to the dancers as it is to the singers.

A complete War Dance finally ends, sometimes after as many as thirty renditions of a song, when there is an absence of nonverbal cues, usually indicating that both singers and dancers are fatigued. When the dance concludes, the dancers retire to the shade where they smoke and talk. The singers likewise smoke and talk and listen to the songs of other song groups. Occasionally, there are giveaways or other announcements between War dances. If the announcer takes too long to conduct a giveaway, dancers and singers become impatient: The dancers begin jingling their leg bells, which is both a cue to the announcer to hurry but also (should he not) a signal to the singers to interrupt the announcer and begin another War dance song. The jingling of bells by one dancer usually en-

Dance at Rosebud, July 4, 1940. The singers are resting in the center of the arbor during the give away. O'Neill Photo. Courtesy Heritage Center, Inc.

courages others to do likewise. An impatient singer may impetuously strike the drum loudly with one or two beats, and it is not unheard of to find a song leader starting up a song at the instant that the announcer has stopped his speaking momentarily to take a breath.

ANALYSIS

Now that I have described the Oglala variant of the War dance, I will provide an analytical framework for what otherwise may appear to be a confusion of shouts, nods, drumbeats, bell ringing, whistling, and ululations. I take my own cue from sociolinguistics, particularly Jakobson's adaptation of communications theory to linguistics (Jakobson 1953, 1960). I regard the powwow as a "communicative event" (Hymes 1974, 9) and the interactions between singers and dancers, as well as the total range of nonverbal cues, as components of this event. The relevant features may be classified systematically according to a "somewhat elaborate version of factors identified in communication theory" (Hymes 1974, 10). There are seven factors: (1) participants, (2) channels, (3) codes, (4) setting, (5) form of message, (6) contents, and (7) event—all of which are necessary to provide an ethnographic account of a communicative event.

1. Participants. For the purpose of this analysis, singers and dancers may be regarded as senders and receivers of information. Auditors and the effect on a third person or party on the senders and receivers is not included.[12] Information may be transmitted in the following ways: (1) between singers, (2) between singers and dancers, (3) between dancers and singers, and (4) between dancers.

2. Channels. The most pronounced channels are drumming, face and body motion, whistling, ululation, and the nonverbal (that is, nonsemantic) segments of the songs (vocables) and nonchoreographic aspects of the dance, namely, bell ringing.

3. Codes. The codes shared by singers and dancers fall into two main categories: (1) oral-aural codes and (2) gestural-visual codes. The oral-aural code may be further subclassified on the basis of the source of nonverbal cues, that is, (a) vocalic and (b) instrumental. The gestural-visual code may also be subdivided on the basis of individual and group nonverbal behavior, that is, (a) kinesic and (b) proxemic.

4. Setting. The Oglala variant of the War Dance may be regarded as the setting, in recognition that other kinds of dances require different kinds of setting—for example, round dances, rabbit dances, victory dances—and that each new setting requires a variation in the interaction between singers and dancers and the drum area and dance area.

5. Form of message. The form of the message has one common denominator: it is nonverbal. The range of nonverbal cues is treated above under channels and codes.

6. The contents. The contents that the message conveys focus on the practical regulation of the War Dance so that singers and dancers may end together on the last beat of the drum. The message also simultaneously conveys attitudes of the singers and dancers, ranging from enthusiasm to indifference in the selection of the song and performance of the singers, on one hand, and the presence of female singers and performance of the dancers, on the other.

7. Event. The event under which all other factors are subsumed is the powwow. Some variations in the channels and

codes may be expected depending on the location of the event, that is, indoors or outdoors.

I will now rearrange the above seven factors hierarchically enabling one to discern the range of variation of nonverbal cues around an Oglala drum. The resultant typology also becomes useful in analyzing other aspects of the powwow, both verbal and nonverbal, musical and nonmusical.[13]

  I. Event: outdoor powwow, Oglala variant
 II. Setting: War Dance
III. Form of message: nonverbal
 IV. Content of message: regulation-evaluation of War Dance
  V. Participants, codes, and channels
   A. Singers (senders) and singers (receivers)
     1. Oral-aural codes
       a. Vocal cues
         i. Vocabalic
         ii. Ornamentative[14]
         iii. Ululative
       b. Instrumental cues
         i. Membranophonic[15]
     2. Gestural-visual codes
       a. Kinesic cues
         i. Facial
         ii. Manual
       b. Proxemic cues
         i. Mobile (female singers)
   B. Singers (senders) and dancers (receivers)
     1. Oral-aural codes
       a. Vocal cues
         i. Vocabalic
         ii. Ornamentative
       b. Instrumental cues
         i. Membranophonic
     2. Gestural-visual codes
       a. None
   C. Dancers (senders) and singers (receivers)
     1. Oral-aural codes
       a. Vocal cues
         i. Ululative (females)
         ii. Ornamentative (males)

      b. Instrumental cues
        i. Areophonic[16]
        ii. Ideophonic[17]
  2. Gestural-visual codes
    a. Kinesic
      i. None
    b. Proxemic
      i. Mobile (male and female)
D. Dancers (senders) and dancers (receivers)
  1. Oral-aural cues
    a. Vocal cues—none
    b. Instrumental
      i. Aerophonic
      ii. Ideophonic
  2. Gestural-visual codes

The above typology accounts for all nonverbal behavior between singers and dancers during a War Dance that both regulates the duration of a dance and simultaneously evaluates it (longer dances are better). A typology based on seven factors in communications theory seems useful not only for discerning the components of a communicative event such as the powwow but also for examining other aspects of the same event. For example, the same typology can be applied to a Round Dance, a Rabbit Dance, or any other musical event. It seems, however, that the typology is also useful for discerning verbal as well as nonverbal components, and musical and nonmusical components of the same event, thus leading to an integrative ethnography of verbal and nonverbal communications of a single communicative event.

CHAPTER 3

COUNTING YOUR BLESSINGS: SACRED NUMBERS AND THE STRUCTURE OF REALITY

THE purpose of this chapter is to examine the phenomenon of sacred or mystical numbers found in all religions of the world.[1] It is examined from the perspective of an anthropologist with a strong conviction that ultimate solutions to problems of human nature reside in laws governing general biological evolutionary principles. My perspective immediately disregards the question, "Neurobiology . . . does it matter?" unless it is posed in a rhetorical sense, and as long as it implies evolutionary neurobiology since most neurobiologists are probably not interested in evolution per se. I further disregard the question because I view culture as an analytical domain that identifies and describes the particular way humans have adapted to the environment biologically. Further implied is the basic biogenetic structuralist position that perceptions of reality are constantly structured and restructured cognitively and affectively through the "functioning of neural structures, which evolved and became progressively elaborated because of the adaptive advantage they conferred on their bearers."[2]

I also examine sacred numbers on the basis of theories of semiotic structuralism on the one hand and evolutionary biology on the other—all this in the middle of a lifelong infatuation with American Indians, with whom I have had the pleasure of studying. A left-brain investment with a right-brain payoff! This ongoing field experience, lasting thirty-nine years, has taught me that ethnography is still alive and well and has further enlightened me to the fact that structuralism and evolutionary biology are simply two aspects of the same analytical process and do, in fact, belong on the same hand. It is probably the right one.

This study, then, is an attempt to integrate some of my own studies of religion in various parts of the world, and in particular on the Pine Ridge Indian Reservation in South Dakota among the Oglala Lakotas (Sioux), with some of the larger questions posed by biosocial anthropology.[3]

In keeping with the sacrality inhered in the number 3 in our own society, this chapter is divided into three parts because, as I shall show, it *feels* good to do so. I will begin by examining the sparse literature on the sociology and anthropology of enumeration, or what Lévi-Strauss in his amazingly brief treatment of the subject calls "numerology."[4] Here I want to demonstrate that so-called symbolic, structural, or semiotic analysis is much more complementary to bioevolutionary theory than opposed to it. Implicitly, I continue to question the utility of making distinctions between biological evolution and cultural evolution, perhaps the major point of criticism of cultural anthropology by sociobiologists and biogenetic structuralists (although I realize the latter may not want to be lumped together any more than cultural anthropologists do). Similarly I want to question whether we should continue to distinguish between "semiotic" structuralism, exemplified by the French sociological tradition, and characteristic of the current works of Mary Douglas, Edmund Leach, Victor Turner, and Claude Lévi-Strauss, and the so-called evolutionary structuralism that finds its major proponents in the Ivy League institutions of the northeastern United States.[5]

Second, I will describe particular numerical relationships, sacred numbers from various societies cited in the literature, and from my own field research among the Oglalas at Pine Ridge. My point of emphasis is that, in the past, social scientists in describing the sacred or mystical numbers of other societies have tended to view numbers or recurring sets of numbers as static models of a society's symbolic representations, relegating numerical systems to the field of *mythological* behavior. In doing so, they have tended to emphasize the importance of single sets of numbers, say three in Christianity, or four among North American Indians. My own perspective is in seeing numerical relationships as dynamic models of symbolic representations, which are equally analyzable from the perspective of *ritual* behavior, and which often involve multiple numerical relationships, or sets of numbers superimposed one upon another. Finally, as such, sacred numbers not only may be analyzed from the perspective of semiotics but as models of process may be useful also to the biogenetic structuralist as another type of equilibration between the central nervous system and the environment.[6]

Another reason sacred numbers may be of some interest to bioevolutionists is that they emerge as both concrete and abstract systems, often making references to parts of the human body in their concrete form. Since numerical systems are counted on the hands and fingers, and by pointing, there is a postulated relationship between handedness and counting. These concrete systems, however, are capable of becoming transformed over time into abstract systems when the names for numbers derived from the concrete system are discarded or otherwise forgotten. Sacred numbers, then, are of interest to the evolutionary neurobiologist particularly from the standpoint of relationships between brain and behavior and to the evolutionists who can profitably view sacred numbers as possible types of mnemonic devices that must have played an important role in human evolution. The point here is that counting may be viewed not only as a means of enumeration but as a form of memorization. Sacred numbers structure reality by inventing it, and recurring sets of numbers preexist for the purpose of structuring reality.[7]

1

In my opinion, the greatest contribution to the study of numeric systems is that of the much maligned and frequently ignored black sheep of French sociology, Lucien Lévy-Bruhl. Despite the fact that Lévy-Bruhl was attacked by his colleagues, an onslaught that continues today, he did in fact write six volumes on so-called primitive mentality, believing that primitives, though capable of participating in rational thought, did not do so, at least not yet, in evolutionary thinking of the times. Instead, primitives "participated" in their belief systems, were at one with them, which Lévy-Bruhl perceived to be different from our own form of rational or logical thinking. Primitives expressed what he called prelogical mentality.

One of these volumes, published in 1910 under the title *Les Fonctions mentales dans les sociétés inférieures* and translated into English in 1926 as *How Natives Think*, devotes a full chapter to "Prelogical Mentality in Relation to Numeration." This is a very exciting chapter because Lévy-Bruhl, in his analysis of numerical systems worldwide, comes to some very important conclusions of interest to evolutionary biologists.[8]

First, he distinguishes between "concrete" and "abstract" systems of numeration, a distinction that Lévi-Strauss follows later in *The Savage Mind*. Concrete systems are those that make reference mainly to parts of the body. Lévy-Bruhl's contention is that primitive peoples are incapable of expressing higher orders of numbers and simply use parts of their body as mnemonic devices for counting. Many of these systems begin with only one or two words, actually translatable or glossed as "one," "two," and then proceed by making reference to the little finger, ring finger, middle finger, and so forth, counting up the arms across the chest and down the other arm and so forth in order to enumerate continuously. There are particularly good examples of these systems from Australia and New Guinea.

For example, in British New Guinea we find the following system in use and reported by James Chalmers:[9]

1 = little finger of left hand
2 = next finger
3 = middle finger
4 = index finger
5 = thumb
6 = wrist
7 = between wrist and elbow

8 = elbow
9 = shoulder
10 = neck
11 = left breast
12 = chest
13 = right breast
14 = right side of neck

Here it should be noted that in the native tongue there is no verbal distinction between 10 and 14, each using the term "neck."

Lévy-Bruhl considered other types of systems that he regarded as half concrete, half abstract.

In the Andaman Islands, a system based on the number 5 was prevalent. There were glosses for numbers 1 and 2, but 3 was glossed as "one more," 4 as "some more," and 5 as "all." These were obvious references to the fingers of one hand.[10]

In the Torres Strait Islands, a base-five principle also obtained, but in a more sophisticated way. For example, 5 was rendered as *nabiget*, 10 as *nabiget nabiget*, 15 as *nabikoko*, and 20 as *nabikoko nabikoko*. In the native language *nabi* means 'all,' 'entirely'; *get* means 'hand'; and *koko* means 'foot.' Thus 5 really meant 'the entire hand' (fingers); 10, 'entire hand [plus] entire hand'; 15, 'entire foot' (toes); and 20, 'entire foot [plus] entire foot.'[11]

On the other hand, abstract systems are those composed of single numbers in a series and combinations, as in our own system, by assigning each an individual or derivative term. One of the major discoveries by those who have worked in the sociology of enumeration is that many abstract systems are based on once-verbalized forms for not only parts of the body but also positions of the fingers and hands in counting. If my analysis of the previous literature is correct, at least some of these systems are asymmetrical; i.e., they begin on the left hand, with the right hand pointing to each of the named fingers to begin the counting. Hence the right hand in one case points to the five fingers of the left from 1 to 5 and then takes over itself from 6 to 10.[12]

For example, it is customary for the Lakota and other sign-talking tribes to use their hands in counting even when verbalizing these numbers. The Lakota begin enumerating with the little finger of the left hand, bending each subsequent finger down with the right hand until it is time to change hands. The number 6 is formed by placing the right thumb next to the left thumb with the other fingers remaining bent, and subsequently each finger on the right hand is raised, 7 falling on the right index finger and so on.[13]

It is my contention that counting as a form of numerical system certainly must have displayed the same tendency for handedness, with the right hand as an active counter and the left hand as a passive one, as other and more recent handedness studies have demonstrated, linking this behavior directly to the hemispheric functions of the brain.[14] Of course, this may be premature, but certainly it is a testable hypothesis that can be examined not only in numerical systems but also in other systems such as the performance of instrumental music. For example, even where coordination is required, there is frequently an asymmetrical relationship between the use of the hands, say, in playing a piano, where generally left-hand acuity is notably lacking, or in playing the guitar, where the right hand actually controls the production of the sound.[15]

I should add that sign language itself is also worth studying from the perspective of active and passive hand signals. For example, in Plains Indian sign language, the signs are either symmetrical or skewed to the right hand, but never to the left.[16]

To return to Lévy-Bruhl: We see that a second matter, somewhat akin to the first, is that, after comparing data on numeration in the anthropological literature, he notes that where abstract numbers do not exist numeration systems simply act as an aid to one's memory. He cites the work of Haddon, who observes that true numerals do not exist among the tribes of the Torres Strait Islands. Of particular concern to Haddon was that the same body part is used to represent more than one number, and it is only the relative position of the body part in the counting system that discriminates one number from another.

Third, Lévy-Bruhl also underscores the fact that mystic numbers fall between 1 and 10 and that all others are simply combinations. He analyzes a numeric system in which binary and trinary based systems are used to express any given number but regards them as examples of "primitive mentality." Today we would consider this the most complex form. As another example, he discusses a peculiar system of the Yorubas in which a principle of subtraction is used; for example, 11, 12, 13, 14, and 15 are formed by adding 10 plus 1, 2, 3, etc., but 16, 17, 18, and 19 are formed by subtracting 4, 3, 2, and 1 from 20. In this system, 70 becomes 20 times 4 minus 10, and 130 becomes 20 times 7 minus 10; this is apparently derived from counting cowrie shells that have been arranged previously in parcels of 5, 20, and 200.[17]

Fourth, and of particular interest in the study of sacred numbers and their relationship to the structuring of reality, Lévy-Bruhl hits upon two ideas, one his own and the other from the works of Bergaigne[18] in India. In his attempt to see primitive numeration systems as exemplary of prelogical mentality, Lévy-Bruhl associates this form of thinking with animal perception, stating that even such domesticated animals as dogs and elephants can detect objects missing from a familiar scenario. Like animal memory, primitive enumerative operations rely on remembering the sum total rather than constituent parts. He states:

> If anything is missing from the sum-total, they instantly perceive it. In the representation so faithfully preserved, the number of persons or things is not differentiated: nothing allows of its being expressed separately. It is none the less perceived qualitatively, or, if you prefer it, *felt*.[19]

In a more contemporary analysis, we might want to consider the affective role that numbers play on the central nervous system, that is, the adaptive advantage of human beings being able to bracket life experiences, particularly threatening and fearful ones, in such a way as too predict the outcomes of unknown circumstances.

But it is Bergaigne who somewhat cryptically announces

that all numbers are equal and comes to the conclusion that the "numbers three and seven, in the general system of Vedic mythology, should be regarded as frameworks prepared before hand, independent of the personalities which may be summoned up to occupy them."[20]

Lévy-Bruhl is fascinated with this analysis and concludes the difference between what he calls mystical numbers and numbers used in arithmetical calculation is that,

> instead of the number depending on the actual plurality of the objects perceived or pictured, it is on the contrary the objects whose plurality is defined by receiving its form from a mystic number decided upon beforehand. Thus the properties of numbers predetermine, as it were, what the multiplicity will be in the collective representations.[21]

Vladimir Propp came to the same conclusion in his study of Russian folktales, a point on which both Roman Jacobson in linguistics and Lévi-Strauss in social anthropology rely, resulting in the structuralist's dictum that form takes primacy over content.[22]

While reexamining these two final points that somehow mystical numbers—although I would have to add that perhaps all numbers serve this function, sacred or secular, or at least potentially are capable of serving this function—have a qualitative attribute; that is, they can be felt, and, second, Bergaigne's point, that these numbers are predetermined. One immediately wants to know who—or what—predetermined them.

2

One of the most widely developed ways of structuring the parts of a whole is simply by counting them. Since this is so fundamental (some might say an elementary way of classifying important ideas and things), the process of numerical structuring must have been with humankind for most of its evolution. One might speculate that human beings learned to count before they learned to speak and that operationalizing combinations of numbers was a prerequisite for becoming human.

Numbers not only have the capacity to connect important configurations of thought but frequently provide a frame within which these fundamental ideas continue for long periods of time. Not only do numbers have digital qualities, but people perceive them as having shapes such as circles to express unity, dyads such as the Chinese symbol for yin and yang, a triangle to express the trinity, a box to symbolize fourness, and so on. It seems that if these numerical configurations can be shaped in specific ways there is a guarantee that they will become instantly embedded in the mind. As such, they will serve as tools by which the meanings behind the shapes will become known, and there will be an additional satisfaction that if the shapes themselves are somehow simple but meaningful they will be remembered much more easily.[23]

There is perhaps nothing sacred in numerical structures, even though all peoples of the world count their blessings arithmetically as well as with hope and sometimes relief. But the same holiness of the trinitarian representation of Christian faith can easily be reinterpreted to form a Marxist dialectic; and, of course, the reverse is true. If a dialectical relationship is one that expresses opposites mediated by the presence of both oppositional qualities—plus as opposed to minus with the mediation of plus/minus—then we can, with little modification of the original Hegelian concept, talk about God the Father opposing God the Son and the mediation between the two by the Holy Ghost. This dialectic is based not on superiority or inferiority of each of the three parts but rather on the belief that God's domain is heaven, while the Son's is earth. The Holy Ghost, of course, mediates between the two locationally; it is capable of occupying both domains.

The number 3 also has been a main unifying factor in the development of the Western intellectual tradition. We are so accustomed to framing ideas into threes that we rarely give it much thought. On the other hand, we are quick to try to understand the same principles as they apply in other cultures using other numerical devices. This foreign unifying system appeals to us, and we expect to somehow learn more from exposure to yin and yang than is readily available in our own trinitarian society with less apparent mysteriousness but with the same force of structural opposition.

It is no wonder that we are struck by the systematic way in which the Lakota classify their entire universe by fours and sevens,[24] as if our own system cannot live up to the elegance of a tetradic and heptadic system. Of course, ours can, but we are more inspired by the Lakota system because we expect that there is knowledge there that we cannot discover in our own less-than-natural society, one constrained by triplicity.

Perhaps what is appealing about Lakota numerical systems is not simply that everything in the natural and cultural universe can be described and classified according to a relatively simple numerical system but that, rather than there being one system, there are in fact two. One of these systems is based on the number 4 and generally relates to what is perceptually all persons, places, and objects in nature—the four directions, the four seasons, the four stages of life, four kinds of living things, four phases of a plant, and so on. The other system is based on the number 7, generally a number related to divisions of what we may call in a Lévi-Straussian sense culture. Empirically, the Lakotas identify most of their social and political divisions as sevens.

Both the number 4 and the number 7 have the capacity to symbolize a sense of natural and cultural fulfillment. When one "reaches" the end of the ritual line, so to speak, one gets off the ritual bus at either of these arithmetical stops. Both numbers not only establish a sense of fullness or completion but are statements of denouement. They are also statements about the future as well as about the past and present. In a sense, there is a hope and safety in numbers that have a definite stop point: the only thing that can happen after reaching 4 or 7 in the natural and cultural counting system is that the series can start over again at 1. There is a comfort that infinity can be controlled; it is cyclical, not ortholinear. In this system, and perhaps all other systems that place a great deal of faith in numbers, the unpredictability of the future is controllable through repetition of the proper rituals and prayers, themselves divided into sets or parts that structure some numerical hope.

I think that these numerical systems, one based on four, the other on seven, should not be seen simply as mutually exclusive categories, one making reference to natural things, the other to cultural things. That would be too simple. The two systems are quite complementary if not mutually dependent. The basic number, of course, is 4, and 7 is partly derived from the basic numerical foundation to which other numbers have been added.

Ethnohistorians tell us that some early explorers found that the Sioux were divided into ten (bands?) and wonder why I did not use the number 10 for my model of Lakota social organization instead of 7. The reason, of course, should be clear even to the novice student of Siouan culture: the model 7 is one that the Lakota people employ even though they have access to the same literature that ethnohistorians consult. The Lakotas—and all other peoples of the world—are interested not so much in the way things are as in the way things *should be*, and the way they should be is perceived as a structure organized into seven constituent parts in a very predictable way. It is the naïve anthropologist or historian who expects to find numerical systems that reflect reality. It is rather reality that is fitted into the numerical system, which preexists as a structuring organizational principle of perceived reality.

Frequently these two numerical systems are imposed upon each other in unusual ways; that is, four and seven coexist with a single ritual performance. In the filling of the pipe, and in placing stones in the Sweat Lodge, there is a conceptual distinction made between four and seven, and seven itself is further seen as a sum of four, two, and one. In this system, the tetradic structure symbolizes the four directions, the dyadic structure represents the opposition Above and Mother Earth, and the monadic structure symbolizes a metaphorical bird, the Spotted Eagle. Of course, these structures are symbolic of what Victor Turner would call multivocality (Turner

Sweat lodge at Pine Ridge. The frame contains sixteen saplings.

1969); they are capable of symbolizing a number of concepts independently and/or simultaneously. The tetradic structure can symbolize any natural category, or metaphor, for the constituent parts of these categories such as colors, birds, animals, and seasons, all of which are paradigmatically related and as such stand as metaphors of the four directions. The dyadic structure can serve to symbolize any contrasting set that is significant in Lakota culture: good and evil, knowledge and ignorance, ancient and modern, left and right, and so forth. The monadic element also symbolizes not only the center of the earth but also the place where the individual *is*, and as such is a metaphor for the individual.

The imposition of one numerical system on the other is not unique and is certainly not limited to the Lakota or other American Indian belief systems. In Western thought also we find complementary numerical systems. For example, in baseball (as Dundes has pointed out), we have the prevalence of an ordering system based on the number 3, but frequently the number 4 serves as a perhaps secondary ordering system whereby we have three strikes but four balls leading to different kinds of denouement, one negative and one positive (you are "out" in the first; you "walk" in the second). This series is repeated, as Dundes tells us, in naming the bases as "first," "second," and "third," but the fourth is "home plate." [25]

Similarly, in Christianity, where again the organizing principle is based mainly on a triadic structure, there is an accommodation, one might say, in which the number 4 is imposed on the number 3. In representational art (despite the inaccurate depiction of historical reality) the cross upon which Christ was crucified is depicted as a cross, that is, an icon, essentially divided into four parts. The attempt to depict the cross ritually and at the same time indicate its trinitarian importance results in the sign of the cross. Whether inscribed in the air, as when a priest applies a ritual blessing on a person, place, or object, or whether directed against oneself by placing the tips of the fingers of the right hand serially on the forehead, chest, left shoulder, right shoulder, there is an essential conflation of two numerical systems that for the time being (that is, for the duration of the ritual) coexist and in doing so emphasize the importance and mutual dependence of the two systems. The process is not unlike the actions of the single musician, say, a West African drummer, who plays a time signature of 4/4 with his right hand on one drum and at the same time plays "against" it with the left hand on a second drum in 3/4 time. The thrill of hearing such polyrhythm is probably analogous to the religious elation one feels at the point of being exposed to the unconscious tension created by the imposition of four on three in the Christian system, or seven on four in the Lakota system. Again by way of emphasis, I believe that it is useful to view sacred numbers as having the capacity to evoke affective behavior, like other symbols, and as such to be *felt*.

There is another quality in these numerical systems, briefly alluded to above, and that is their capacity to express a dynamic. The various symbolic representations of these numerical systems are usually thought of as static, for example, the *cangleška wakan* 'sacred circle' or 'hoop,' a circle inscribing a cross, symbolic of the entire universe, as well as other paintings or three-dimensional representations such as a crucifix or sacred pipe. They are also capable of expressing movement and viability. Numbers that are sacred are generally those that somehow mark the end, the finality of a sacred process expressed in prayer, songs, and ritual. It is the sacred number that through its emphasis on the termination of a series implies the processes leading up to its termination. The sacred number 4 is important because of the implicit series that has created it . . . 1, 2, 3 . . . . The number 7 is sacred because of the internal constructs and a respective serialization that has given them structure: 4, 2, 1 . . . .

Since understanding this dynamic attribute of the numerical system is critical to understanding the very concept that is symbolized in the number, let me provide some ethnographic examples. In the most fundamental sense, there are no people in the world who are not animists, that is, who do not believe there is something that gives rise to the living organism that contains it and that somehow survives this organism when it perishes. *Animism,* of course, comes from the Latin *anima;* in English this concept is called soul. Despite the ubiquity of the ideas of soul, there is no worldwide agreement on the nature of soul or, numerically speaking, just how many souls a living organism has. There is also no agreement on just what kind of living organisms are supposed to contain the various numbers of souls, or aspects of one soul. As a convention, however, one based on a rigid interpretation of the word, animists are usually depicted as "primitive" people who believe that even rocks and trees and animals and birds have souls.

Animism may be contrasted with still another term, *animalism,* similarly derived from the Latin, but by convention identifying those persons who believe that human beings are just another form of animal having no spiritual quality, that is, no *anima.* Animalists are usually defined as atheists and sometimes as scientists, although certainly not all scientists are animalists.

Despite the fact that in English we have a conventional

Latin term that gives rise to two quite opposite ideas, the
Lakota people, who are usually called animists (by both animalists and people who profess belief in the Judaeo-Christian
religion), do not have the same kind of convention. The Lakota
tradition has it that all animate beings (the redundancy is in-
tentional) are born and die and in the process pass through
what by analogy might be called four states of individuation.
Each individual comes into a being as the result of (1) having
a potentiality for being, (2) transforming this potentiality
through birth into an essence that is independent of the body,
(3) providing continuous evidence that this essence exists,
and (4) finally providing evidence that the essence independent of the corporeal existence continues to exist after death,
therefore freeing its potentiality to inhere in another (potential) organism and begin the process all over, ad infinitum, in
what we in English understand to be a system of reincarnation.

When the old Lakota medicine men spoke of this fourfold
soul, they used the terms (1) *šicun*, (2) *tun*, (3) *ni*, and (4) *nagi*,
respectively. These states have been variously described as
constituting a belief in four souls, or at least four aspects of
one soul. Most explanations have come from scholars whose
own traditions require that each person have one soul, and
every other system is simply regarded as a variation on that
theme. If a Lakota were writing a book on Euro-American
souls, he might come to the conclusion that we were somehow deficient because we thought in terms of "one" soul
without any reference to process—unreasonable by Lakota
standards.

If we regard these four states as parts of a process, parts
that are named and stand as separate but related components
in a structural system, then the Lakota concept of soul (as we
may continue to call it for purposes of explanation) is much
easier to understand. The terms are tied together as parts of a
descriptive process that demarcates stages in the coming-into-
being-and-dying process of each individual. I offer a crude
but perhaps telling analogy (recognizing the danger of analogy as well as its power), which, by way of emphasis, I must
state is my own and is not (except perhaps by coincidence) a

Lakota concept. The analogy is that of the production of fire. The beginning assumption is that the source of production is finite. Let us begin by assuming that in the universe there is a limited but constant supply of sparks that will be called upon to begin the ignition process. Who or what calls upon the sparks is really not important for this analogy, although subsequently we may want to assign this task to a Lakota concept, *taku škanškan* 'that which makes things move; creates energy.'

In addition to this finite number of sparks, there is a variety of tinder waiting to be ignited. For the sake of making the analogy real, let us see this tinder as various kinds of dry leaves, small twigs, and other natural, ignitable substances. We assume that once the spark ignites the tinder there will be a flame, and this flame will last for a certain period of time, after which it will transform itself into smoke, the latter being an unequivocal symbol of fire. If we were to name these four stages or, more properly, the potentiality of the creation of three stages, by equating them with the Lakota terms, they would correspond as follows:

Fire	Soul
spark	*šicun*
tinder	*tun*
flame	*ni*
smoke	*nagi*

Continuing the analogy, we might want to name the four separate but related parts of this process simply *fire*, just as we are inclined to name the four separate but related parts of the Lakota concept *soul*. In reality, the Lakota have no general name for soul except those conventions that have been translated by missionaries, usually *woniya*, from *wo* 'noun marker'; *ni* 'life, breath'; and *ya* causal suffix 'to create, make', i.e., 'that which makes breath, or life'. In this case, the missionary convention corresponds with the English word 'spirit' whose Latin derivation gives us a wide semantic range, for example, 'breath, courage, vigor, the soul, life' itself derived from *spirare* 'to breathe, to blow'.

In the past, scholars struggled to interpret the parts of the whole independently: *šicun* is 'potentiality'; *tun* is 'giving birth'; *ni* means 'life' or 'breath'; and *nagi* means 'ghost'. These interpretations are only partly convincing when we think of them as static concepts, but when we look at their interrelationships and dynamic quality, the parts blend neatly into an interpretation emphasizing the whole life process as one in which immortality is achieved through reincarnation. The sacrality of the number 4, then, is certainly one based on process rather than on simple categorization.

But one need not turn only to metaphysical concepts to see how the number 4 implies the unfolding, the development, the evolution of important events. Take, for example, a more visible form or ritual—dance. There are in Lakota ritual a number of choreographic patterns marked by the number 4. In the traditional *ceȟohomni wacipi* 'dance around the kettle' or 'kettle dance', the dancers, after raising their hands to the kettle filled with dog meat in an act of salutation, begin dancing around the kettle four times. After completing this movement, they dance in place as several of them, armed with forked sticks, charge the kettle. Three times they charge the kettle, the fourth time stabbing the choice morsels of meat with their spears.

In the *wiwanyang wacipi* 'gaze at the sun' or 'sun dance', we find countless references to the number 4 as an organizing principle for a longer and more complex ritual. When the sacred pole has been found, four virgins each strike the pole four times with axes before it is felled. On the journey back to the Sun Dance camp, the people carrying the pole stop four times to rest. When the pole is to be erected, the men in charge do so by resting three times as they raise the pole, the fourth time heaving the pole into its proper position.

During the actual performance of the Sun Dance, the Sun Dance leader instructs all of the dancers to face each of the four directions during the course of the daily ordeal. During one part of the dance, they dance four times up to the pole and finally grasp it to pray. At each rest period, a man or a woman, or both, is selected to take a pipe and offer it to the

The sweat-lodge ceremony during the Sun Dance at Pine Ridge, August, 1966. The fire tender hands in a ladle of water during one of four ceremonial recesses. Photo by Paul Steinmetz, S.J. Courtesy Heritage Center, Inc.

head singer. If the singer accepts the pipe, it means that the singing will stop, and the dancers may rest in the shade. There is a peculiar way in which the dancers present the pipe to the head singer. The dancers dance up to him holding their pipes in both hands in front of their chests. Three times they dance forward and present the pipe to the head singer, who feigns at taking it but refuses to accept it. At this point, the dancers dance backward and again dance forward to present the pipe. Three times the pipe is refused, but the fourth time it is accepted, and the singers stop singing just as soon as the head singer has taken the pipe. The dancers then file off the dance ground to rest.

The number of ceremonies and rituals we can use to analyze the significance of the sacred numbers is unending and suggests a new meaning. All of these variations tell us that numbers are not simply static but that staticity is only one dimension of numbers that can be viewed equally from a dynamic perspective. Numbers are at once a statement about

Sun Dancers at Rosebud, ca. 1920s. The dancer on the left carries a sacred hoop symbolic of the four directions.

time and space, about synchrony and diachrony, about states of movement and motionlessness. Numbers have the capacity to analyze and at the same time synthesize and for this reason serve as one of the greatest of symbolic vehicles; they are singularly powerful messages because of their multidimensionality. Numbers are at once paradigm and syntagm, metaphor and metonymn.

In cosmology as well as ritual, we find exhaustive references to the number 4 in both static and dynamic representations. For example, if we look at other symbols of the Four Winds, we can see that new modes of analysis can help unlock potential meaning. In the past we would have been likely on "logical" grounds to see the members of the Four Winds—West, North, East, and South—as constituting a category. At the same time, the relationships between the directions and, say, colors, animals, and birds that symbolize each of the respective directions were syntagmatically related. A syntagmatic chain hypothetically would be produced by the association of, say, West Wind, representing the paradigm "direction"; fall representing the paradigm "season"; black representing the paradigm "color" associated with the direction; buffalo representing the "animal" symbolizing the direction, etc. The entire series may be schematized in the following way:

Direction	Season	Color	Animal	Bird
West	Fall	Black	Blacktail deer	Swallow
North	Winter	Red	Buffalo	Magpie
East	Spring	Yellow	Whitetail deer	Crow
South	Summer	White	Elk	Meadowlark

The above schema may be considered the Western inclination to arrange topically and paradigmatically, that is, into things that go together. It produces a group of static categories. From the Lakota point of view, however, the schema makes more sense if we view it in the following way:

The Sun Dance. From a painting by Lakota artist Andrew Standing Soldier. The traditional arbor was constructed of twenty-eight uprights. Copyright 1949 by C. E. Engle.

1	2	3	4
West	North	East	South
Fall	Winter	Spring	Summer
Black	Red	Yellow	White
Blacktail deer	Buffalo	Whitetail deer	Elk
Swallow	Magpie	Crow	Meadowlark

From this perspective, we see that all members of paradigm 1 are interchangeable—that is, in the language of semiotics, they are metaphorically related—while the relationships expressed between paradigmatic sets express metonymical relationships. The point is, in the first schema, there is a tendency to see each paradigmatic set as static, while in the second schema there is a sense of movement. The two schemas are, of course, two aspects of a singular analytical perspective, a perspective based on the notion of a two-dimensional rather than a one-dimensional model. One model produces a static or synchronic representation of the number 4; the second produces a dynamic or diachronic representation.

The second schema also represents what we might regard as a mechanism for breaking the mythical code. Any reference to a singular member of a paradigmatic set is implicitly a reference to all other members of the set (by definition) as well as a reference to the relationship between all four paradigmatic sets. Hence, when a medicine man sings that he is calling a "red stone friend," he is really making a reference to a totality whose aid may be sought by addressing only one of its parts. "Red stone," then, is really a referential marker that signifies the north, winter, buffalo, and so on. Any reference to one member of the set is a reference to all of them. Therefore, a prayer or song that addresses specifically, say, the magpie, a red stone, a whitetail deer, and summer has in fact made a general reference to the four directions.

We should not be so dazzled by analysis, however, that we overlook the quality of fulfillment in sacred numbers—that, in fact, a recitation of the numerical components of the series does lead somewhere. For example, in the creation story, we find metaphorical references to personified gods whose actions result in the creation of a viable universe from a static matrix. The investment of movement in static objects ultimately causes the creation of the universe as the Lakota now see it. During the process, a quadripite plan unfolds in which (1) days and nights are distinguished, (2) the month is established, (3) the year and the seasons (that is, space) are established, leading up to the present "time" period, the fourth generation, which is (4) the present time.

Another symbol underscores the sense of fulfillment inherent in the number 4, even though the symbol itself is a highly negative one, in the form of an apocalyptic story. In it the old Lakota envision the state of affairs of the current universe as symbolized by a buffalo who is literally on its last leg. In the story, the buffalo starts out with four legs and thick hair. Over time, the buffalo begins to lose its hair and ultimately three of its legs. When the buffalo is totally bald and has lost its fourth leg, the world as we know it will come to an end. There is some sense of optimism, though, because the demise of the buffalo will lead to a spiritual reincarnation, and the universe will start all over again—the next time being, it is hoped, more favorable for the Lakota.

The number 4 also should be seen as a means of classifying contemporary ideas relevant to Lakota culture as well as to old traditions. This is perhaps proof that the system of classification is important rather than the things that are classified; that is, the relationship between persons, places, and things is deemed important rather than the persons, places, and things themselves. To see one example of the viability of the system, we need only look at certain relationships that have been made between the directional color system and the concept of "race."

Currently, younger Lakota see a relationship between west = black, north = red, east = yellow, and south = white, and a rather arbitrary classification of human "races" based on old-fashioned scientific and folk notions of "great races of mankind," a scientific position no longer acceptable.

In this new use of the sacred colors, black is equated with black people; red with Indians; white with Europeans; and yellow with undifferentiated Orientals.

Whether scientifically acceptable, which it is not, or even acceptable to traditional religion, which old Lakota claim it is not, this is a clear demonstration that the numerical system takes precedence over the objects it seeks to classify and explain. It is simply an elegant way of explicating a very complex system of relationships. It is, of course, conjectural whether all things in nature may be "inherently" divided into components of four. But from the Lakota viewpoint, all things in culture may be classified by their "natural" proclivity to confine, constrain, and even squeeze things that are meaningful to them into units of four.

One would ask, in a culture where even the most significant concepts of the universe are governed by such forces as spirits who enjoy a good laugh, what is the consequence of playing what must seem to people outside Lakota culture as a frivolous game of numbers? The answer to outsiders must be that it is perhaps a habitual means of explaining the universe and in the process adding a sense of cogency and predictability to an otherwise unknowable environment. It is a tradition no less significant than others based on other numerals. For the Western analyst, the system of classification precedes the means of classification. For the Lakota, they are one and the same.

3

To judge from the previous statements in the ethnographic field, it might be concluded that sacred numbers provide a framework for symbolizing all that is moral in a society. It is not so much what is said or what is enacted but the predictable number of times that something occurs or recurs that makes human beings feel good, feel appropriate, or feel some sense of control over the very environment that often intimidates them since "the human brain strives to remove as much uncertainty as possible."[26] Where the human ability to experience the world without being able to understand its causes, in the so-called zone of uncertainty, where religion has been invented by the human brain in interaction with the environment to account for these disparities, abstract systems such as numbers, serving as perhaps the best example of a structuring principle simply because they are devoid of content, must have arisen as a sine qua non of evolutionary adaptation.

Hence in American society it is not only the blessed trinity that is a statement about particular morality, although in itself, the mere mention of these triadic relationships is understood as a moral statement leading people into affective action. "The Three Bears" may well serve as a secular version of this morality. It is not the fact that they are three bears—any animal would suffice. It is not the fact that things are hot, cold, hard, soft: they are *just right* because each scenario is set up in an anticipated sequence of events that is *felt* to be right, *felt* to be appropriate, *felt* to be final by those brought up in the system. There is something immoral about jokes told about Catholics and Jews, or Catholics and Protestants; but jokes that include a Catholic, a Protestant, and a Jew are not only appropriate—they are funny.

Finally, the idea that all numbers between 1 and 10 are capable of being mystic and Bergaigne's remarkable discovery that all numbers are equal bring us to the possibility of viewing numbers—or rather numerical categories—as dynamic, structuring principles rather than static, discrete categories. Hence, out of a minimal—one is tempted to say finite— number of integers an infinite number of meaningful combinations can be formed. The parallel here is striking in the relationship in linguistics between phonemes (minimal units of sound), which are held to be of a finite number in any natural language, and the utterances of speech, which are seen to be infinite. One is tempted, then, to see a broad parallel between the structuring principle of numerical categories and other biosocial phenomena such as kinship terminological systems that also structure principles, and these principles or models also have been reduced from a countless number of systems known worldwide to a relative few.[27] The idea, then, of reducing these principles to a common point of mediation, a common point of origin, a common cause, does receive wide and favorable acceptance by both the structuralist who follows Lévi-Strauss in attributing the causation of the structuring principles to the structure and function of the brain and mind (in a process leading one might say from the top down) and the evolutionary neurobiologist who views the same relationships between brain and behavior, whether mythological or ritual, from the bottom up. They both meet head on, so to speak, in the middle of the brain. The question becomes: Which came first, the brain or the dialectic?

Although there is a perfect logic in separating the two kinds of structuralism—semiotic on the one hand, and evolutionary on the other—we should not fall into the trap that our antecedents have, to wit, separating nature from nurture or in anthropological terms, biological evolution from cultural evolution. The difference between synchrony and diachrony, after all, is never that sharp, and we should heed the semioticians, beginning with Ferdinand de Saussure,[28] who said that synchrony and diachrony can be seen as two aspects of the same phenomenon differentiated by theoretical interests rather than empirical reality. We should also see diachrony and synchrony as being mutually interdependent rather than mutually exclusive categories.

It would seem, however, that the study of numbers, the process of numeration, and the numerical categories that I have called sacred numbers are subject to analysis not so much as categories but as processes. As I have shown in my data, sacred numbers are acted out as well as spoken about. They may be viewed then from the perspective of ritual as much as from the more usual viewpoint of myth. If this is the case, any semiotic, structural, or symbolic study of numbers should greatly assist the biogenetic structuralist. Sacred numbers, or any generally recognized combinations of numbers prevailing in a given culture over long periods of time, certainly can be viewed as a form of *ritual behavior* that somehow mediates between the environment and the individual. In particular, the idea of *equilibration* seems appropriate to describe this interaction between the central nervous system and the environment.

I will end on a note of emphasis. I contend that it is possible to understand numerical systems as essentially one type of system that has the capacity to transform in structuralist terms a finite number of building blocks, analogous to phonemes in language, into an infinite number of numerical sets and derivations of these sets. As we have seen, sacred numbers are limited—from 1 to 10—and these limited numbers are probably themselves developed from constructs based on binary oppositions formed by contrasting one set with another (rather than one integer with another). I would think that these numerical systems would be of interest to brain and behavior researchers since our old, often-ignored and much-maligned friend Lévy-Bruhl has shown, although in different times and under different circumstances (all quite respectable), that numerical systems often correlate with brainedness.

We have certainly reached, in Kuhn's sense, a new paradigm in biosocial thinking, although it has been a long and arduous fight, and we must continue to be mindful of the danger in celebrating Pyrrhic victories. The question, Neurobiology—does it matter? becomes superfluous. The real question is, Can we continue to discuss the analytical category called culture in any meaningful way without accepting a priori the relationship between human brain and human behavior?

CHAPTER 4

SACRED ART AND THE CULTURATION OF NATURE

> Though human ingenuity may make various inventions
> which, by the help of various machines, answer the same
> end, it will never devise invention more beautiful, nor
> more simple, nor more to the purpose than nature does; be-
> cause in her inventions nothing is wanting and nothing is
> superfluous.
> —Leonardo da Vinci (quoted in Cooper 1965, 3)

> [Painting] finds its materials in nature: colors are given be-
> fore they are used, and language bears witness to their de-
> rivative character through the terms that describe the most
> subtle shades—midnight blue, peacock blue, petrol blue;
> sea green, jade green; straw color, lemon yellow; cherry
> red, etc. In other words, colors exist in painting only be-
> cause of the prior existence of colored objects and beings.
> —Claude Lévi-Strauss (1969b, 19)

A continuing problem in the philosophy of art, one that
affects anthropological and historical perspectives on the
human need to create material things, images, reflections—
copies, if you will—of his ideas as well as of his natural universe, is to what extent it is possible to provide an adequate
definition of art that will allow students of human nature and
human behavior to compare, say, the works of Michelangelo
and Rodin to those of, say, an anonymous Lakota hide painter
or pipe carver.[1] Stated more succinctly: Is it possible to con-
ceive of a universal definition of art? Or must we be content
with a multitude of definitions, all of which change dramatically, depending on one's social and cultural background?

I think the Western intellectual tradition is not yet ready to
equate such diverse artistic techniques or the values associ-

ated with them. It is largely owing to the fact that Art, written with a capital *A*, does not exist outside highly ethnocentricized boundaries, whereas art, or more properly arts, written with a small *a*, in its plural form, transects all ethno- and sociocentric perimeters. This is to underscore the fact that Art writ large, ironically, always must be defined in a narrow way, and this limited definition must always imply a sense, or relative if not absolute, in the eyes of the definers—of superiority. One may go so far as to say that Art writ large may be contrasted ultimately only with art, i.e., the art of other people, and may partly exist on the basis that those people who define art believe that their creations are superior to those of other cultures.

Only recently has the contemporary art of non-Western peoples of New Guinea, Africa, and Native North America, among others, been allowed in Art museums—and here I contrast the latter with natural history museums. In the past it has been customary to place the art of non-Western peoples side by side with stuffed animals and the skeletal remains of dinosaurs. These arts have been only recently allowed in museums such as the Metropolitan and the Whitney in New York because they have first been classified by members of the Western art world as "primitive Art" and are, therefore, somehow worthy of being viewed by a critical if not curious public. Here I should add that, in addition to so-called primitive Art, the "cruder" peoples of the Western art world also produce something *less* than Art writ large and presumably something *more* than primitive Art, and this is the so-called *folk art* that has become so popular in galleries and boutiques. It is quite clear that the way we traditionally classify art is simply an extension of the way we classify people, and the whole scheme smacks of the classificatory system made famous by numerous social theorists living in the mid-nineteenth century. Sir Edwin B. Tylor of England and Lewis Henry Morgan reflected current Victorian perceptions in seeing all of humankind as culturally evolving through three stages of development, namely, savagery, a period characterized by hunting and gathering; barbarism, a period characterized by the development of agriculture and ceramic industries; and, finally, civilization, whose hallmark was the invention of writing. Thus we have a popular view of primitive art, folk art, and Art writ large as, in effect, structural analogs of savagery, barbarism, and civilization.

Although these theories are rejected by most anthropologists except perhaps those in the Soviet Union, where people like Morgan have been made heroes mainly because this kind of theorizing nicely complements Marxist theories of historical and economic determinism, the ideas are still very much alive among laymen and are very much, consciously or unconsciously, carried over into other specific cultural domains such as art and religion, the second also being one that defines itself hierarchically and in terms of contrasting superior and inferior poles along the same old savage-to-civilized continuum.

Some of the problems in the classification of American Indian art are universal. For example, there seems to be a universal need to classify art not only from primitive to civilized, or Western versus non-Western, but also along lines of schools of art—cubism, dadaism, impressionism, surrealism, etc., most of which are attributed to the influences of great artists. Another problem of classification is plaguing various types of art, even in the Western tradition, and that is the classification according to medium of expression. We therefore find a need to separate watercolor from oil and both from pencil, and all of them from sculpture, which itself is further subdivided according to elements such as clays or stone or wood or metal and so forth. As if we were not perplexed enough, there is the continuing problem of where to place woven things and knotted things and glued things and paper things. What is perhaps worse in our never-ending need to classify, divide, and further subdivide is our often hypocritical acceptance of American Indian art as long as the medium conforms to an accepted Western medium; that is, a buffalo painted on a buffalo hide that is pictographic in form and is colored with a bone brush that picks up mineral and vegetal paints mixed in a ceramic bowl is primitive! But a buffalo painted on a canvas that is realistic in form and is colored with a sable brush that picks up oil paint from a palette is art! Or, at least, potentially Art.

There is a similar kind of hypocrisy, the kind we hear verbalized at gallery openings and cocktail parties, when an Oscar Howe painting such as his *Sioux Rider*[2] is unveiled revealing a warrior carrying a shield and lance—upon a horse with no feet—and one remarkably resembling Amos Bad Heart Bull and other "Unknown Sioux Artists"[3] of the past. The Howe is therefore pictographic in form. Yet it is dubbed Art with a capital *A* without the slightest hesitation. Again, as if our hypocrisy is not already strained and near the point of breaking, one of Oscar Howe's more cubistic paintings, such as *Woman Dancer,*[4] is destined to be evaluated not as a stage in the development of an artist who is also Sioux (as would be attributed to, say, Picasso). Rather, it would be evaluated as an Indian painting done by a Sioux who is also an artist.

Lest I be misconstrued here, I use Oscar Howe as an example because he has many appealing styles—he does not fit into a niche, and I think he can be compared more easily to Picasso than to another "Unknown Sioux Artist."

A further question confronting all art forms, one that is part of the problem of typology, is, How do we differentiate art(s) from craft(s), given, in fact, that we can define either one of them adequately? The real question, of course, is, Why did we develop a society that insists on arguing over the difference between the two, since the definition of each must always be provisional or operational? Perhaps it may boil down to differentiating arts from crafts on the basis of what the artist or craftsman wants defined. As ridiculous as this may sound, it is no more untenable than the current squabblings over the definitions of each.

Before I continue, let me briefly mention one more hypocrisy, the sad revelation that today most art from most societies is defined not by artists (or craftsmen) but, in fact, by art critics and art dealers who set priorities and prices. The inflation of prices over the years clearly indicates that art cannot be defined without some reference to economics and particularly capitalistic forms of economics. In the process of inventing art, dealers have turned what was once symbolic of cooperation into the trademark of competition. Along with government agencies such as the Indian Arts and Crafts Board and the Institute for American Indian Art, dealers have helped create the illusion of individualism and in the process have attempted—unknowingly—to demystify and thus secularize American Indian art. One does not participate in, react to, or dwell on the face of art today as much as look at the obverse side to see the name of the artist. This practice, to me, is a false comparison of arts—false not only where American Indian art is concerned but where all art is concerned. Art is not alone, however, because contemporary literature, if I may use the term, such as *Hanta Yo* and a host of other nonbooks, has been well accepted by the public because it is the product of multinational corporation marketing strategies rather than something that has an aesthetic appeal or fulfills a human need. The question raised over all these media is not so much whether they are pseudo-Indian as whether they are pseudo-art?[5]

The major problem, then, with trying to compare or somehow otherwise evaluate the works of the classic artists of the Western world and the classic artists of, say, an American Indian tradition is that usually both genres of art are compared on the basis of technological achievement (and implicitly "progress"). Here I would like to attempt another kind of comparison of these art forms, a process that is quite commonly acknowledged in anthropology but hardly ever from the perspective of history or philosophy of art. This approach may best be called a structural-functional approach, and it is an idea I would like to discuss because the terms "structure" and "function" are employed in a number of different ways as one moves from one discipline to the next.

By a structural approach to art I refer to the view that art exists only in a context. Unlike proponents of some philosophies of art, I do not—I cannot—as an anthropologist speak of art for art's sake, and I cannot speak of art in any absolute sense. Structurally speaking, art although made up of a lot of parts—form and color, for example—is also part of a larger social and cultural context. This context differs from one society to the next because environments—the flora, fauna, and other people that coexist—differ. There are, then, two structural levels of art in any given society: (1) the relationship between the elemental parts of art—form, shapes, colors, and (2) the relationship between art forms and the remainder of society—that is, the relationship between visual representations, such as paintings and sculpture, and religion, politics, economics, and so forth. Structure always refers to the parts of the whole and how they fit together.

Function, on the other hand, means how the parts work, once fitted to the whole. How do they operate? What do people do with them? An advantage (some would say a disadvantage) is that one does not necessarily require any sense of history (or development, or "progress") to compare arts from various time periods and geographic areas when a structural-functional approach is employed. One of the reasons why it has been difficult to define art universally or compare art from one historical period with that of another is that the basis of evaluation has always been limited to a materialistic approach, i.e., the state of the technology.

Another problem of evaluating and comparing art has to do with the need to impose ideas and terms that are decidedly born of the Western intellectual tradition, a tradition that places a great deal of trust in the presumed universality of such notions as beauty and a distrust in the universality of the idea of the aesthetic.

Part of the reason why in the past Indian art has been excluded from Art writ large is that it was deemed to be functional—in another sense of the word. Here, of course, I am referring to the banal notion that the difference between American Indian art and other kinds of Western arts is that the former is always functional while the latter are always aesthetic—as if the two terms "functional" and "aesthetic" are always somehow mutually exclusive. I would like to point out quickly that there is no reason to assume this is true. But the idea has been so firmly embedded in our own thinking and in our own literature, the normal response—when one hears the words "primitive" or "functional"—is Pavlovian.[6]

Those familiar with North American Indian art (and the same would hold for any non-Western art) will remember that this kind of creative expression is not regarded as true art because it is "functional." Stated another way, it has always been implied that among Indians there is no sense of the aesthetic—only a sense of pragmatism resulting in a multitude of weapons, cooking utensils, clothing, costumes, dwellings, modes of locomotion and transportation, and other functional objects to which are added various kinds of decoration or ornamentation. Often decoration is seen to enhance the practicality or functionality of the object—adding, for example, a certain kind of efficacy or power, usually of a mystical or supernatural type, making the arrow fly straighter and faster by means of a few daubs of paint or a well-manicured feather. Again, the implication is that among the "primitive" there is a certain "primitive mentality," as Lévy-Bruhl would say,[7] that has made some peoples of the world believe that by expressing themselves in form and color, in single or multidimensional media, they could somehow make their wildest visions come true. Thus in Lakota art, red paint makes the object sacred! Perhaps as a better example, look back to the description and analysis of the cave paintings of, say, Lascaux, where it always seems "apparent" that the figures of human beings and animals have been drawn on the walls in the literally dim past for religious reasons. (But how would anyone know that, since the artists of that period have been dead for as long as 40,000 years?) Thus in North American Indian art, it has always been suggested that what is really significant is that it is magical, or better, I think, religious. There is always a notion that when an Indian decorates some common tool the act of decorating it as well as the new form and colors that are created in the process will make the tool more auspicious than it might have been if it had been left unadorned.

As I mentioned before, the functionality of "primitive" art is implicitly, if not explicitly, contrasted with a sense of aes-

The interior of a tipi containing various objects of art. Photo by H. Morelli. Author's collection.

thetics associated with art of the Western world. The term "aesthetic," however, is perhaps even more abstract and more difficult to define than art itself because it relies on a decidedly Western notion of "beauty," a term, and a concept, that does not exist in most languages and cultures of the world. Let us look for a moment at some of our Western definitions of art to see just where these notions fit, and here I am paraphrasing most of the standard dictionary definitions, many of which will be familiar.

First, art is a system of rules designed for procuring some scientific, aesthetic, or practical result, also for achieving mastery of these rules and, by extension, constituting a branch of learning to be studied in order to be applied. Also, art is a facility resulting from practice, dexterity—hence power. Now I think that these definitions do not preclude American Indian art from being counted among the "true" arts of the world. That art is equally well described when Byron (in *The Corsair*) says: "Still sways their souls with that commanding *art* / That dazzles, leads, yet chills the vulgar heart." Or when Ruskin (in *Queen of the Air*) writes, "While manufacture is the work of the hands, art is the work of the whole spirit of man,"—a decidedly religious definition of art, I think.

But we do find it more difficult to admit American Indian art into the art galleries and free it from the ethnographic and natural history museums when we define art as "the embodiment of beautiful thought in sensuous forms," a definition that is eloquent and beauteous but hardly applies to the likes of a cherry pounder or scalping knife.

In describing and defining art from the perspective of beauty, it is simply not good enough to say that beauty is in the eyes of the beholder because where the concept of beauty holds, as it does in our western world, beauty—that is, art in its aesthetic *or* functional form—has been defined for individuals by their culture long before those individuals were born. Beauty or art or aesthetic or functionality—all are concepts that come into existence not in any absolute sense (therefore, speaking strictly from an anthropological perspective, there can never be an art for art's sake), but rather as a consensus of what society—people—invest in these concepts. Because people are born into different cultures and speak different languages and are thrust into different kinds of environments, it is unlikely that there will ever be agreement from a purely materialistic position on just what art is or what art does; the same can be said about religion.

Any useful and universal definition of art must for the time being ignore the usual referents of art—form, color, dimension, genre, style, technique—and concentrate on those common features of art outside its cultural context. We are hardpressed to do this because it is foreign to our way of thinking about art and, I might add, to our way of thinking about religion. We must, in short, stop defining art and religion in their own terms.

And, of course, from an anthropological point of view, a point of view that seeks to understand similarities as well as differences in cultures, art and religion are very much alike. One common point is that both seek to elevate the human being above other animal species. Many animals sing—make some kind of repetitive sound—and many animals dance— repeat certain kinds of physical behaviors in, say, their court- ship patterns. But (as far as we know) only human beings manufacture or create tributes to themselves as well as to those supernaturals whom they perceive to have had some hand in their origin. From a strict cultural-evolutionary point of view, all art is sacred because, as I suggest in my title, art, like religion, is a cultural means of not only experiencing re- ality but controlling it. Art and religion are, as Lévi-Strauss has stated, means by which human beings underscore the fact that they are at once a part of nature but at the same time *apart*—separate from—nature.[8]

Art, like religion, helps people define time and space; in this regard, art and religion are inseparable. Old things, once locked into a piece of marble or painted on a hide, increase in value not so much because they are art as because they are old. They help demark history itself by freezing a famous per- son or a famous event—realistically or impressionalistically— so that it survives forever, and this survival quality is what makes the art important and valuable. Religion—perhaps all religions—operates precisely the same way, as even the Latin base for religion acknowledges—*religere*, 'to tie back.' Things then become deserving of worship not because they are sa- cred but because they are old; they have persisted over great periods of time. It is difficult for us to distinguish clearly be- tween beholding an art form and beholding a god, or between beholding the image of a god and the god itself. Stated an- other way, art is itself an expression of religion because the emotions expressed in art and the emotions expressed in reli- gion spring from the same human needs. Thus we are asked to be silent when we enter the Sistine Chapel or a sweat lodge not only because they are houses of prayer but equally because they are cultural delineations of time and space—both are man-made, manufactured of the very same natural elements from which man strives to separate himself.

Art has the same qualities that Rudolph Otto[9] has described for religion: a *mysterium*, or magnetic force drawing humans to it, and, at the same time, a *tremendum*, a repelling force that makes the object so much the more curious, and finally a *fasinans*, a preoccupation with the form and color and also with the dualistic nature, which makes the object worthy of study or worthy of valuation. How much nature also fits this dual quality, constantly attracting us to it while at the same time forcing us to define ways in which we are superior to or at least different from it. Perhaps the contrast between nature and culture, and ambivalent feelings about where humans fit into this opposition, account for nature being so important as a subject for artistic representation as well as for so-called pantheistic religion, all religions being somewhat pantheistic despite the term's usual association with "primitive" peoples.

Returning to an alternative method of defining art, one that is lacking in the philosophy of art, I wish to consider the following ways in which all arts of the Western and non-Western world show similarities. I should begin by saying that, if there are any universal features of art and religion or art and music, or any of the expressive media, this should be so because the expressive parts of culture (art, music, dance, poetry, and religion) are really reflections on the relationship between human beings as a species and the environment in which they find themselves. Lévi-Strauss has stated that art and music are quite different because the elements of art may be found in the natural environment—form and color, for example—but the elements of music are more like the elements of myth and other forms of speech; that is to say, they are the reflections of the human mind itself. I am afraid that I have to disagree with Lévi-Strauss here because I believe, as many musicians from disparate cultures believe, that the elements of music—for example, rhythm and tonality—are likewise found in the natural environment. The Indians tell you that the inspiration for music lies in the wind sounding through the trees, through the calls of birds, the throbbing of the prairie chickens in the leks or drumming areas as they are called.[10] And I firmly believe that what humans do in both art and music, and in religion, is simply and discretely harness various phenomena associated with the natural world and *culturate* them—a formal way of saying that humans employ natural means for cultural ends. Stated another way, nature is humanized through art, through music, and the other expressive modes, and through religion: One might even go so far as to say that all of the expressive aspects of culture are religious, or perhaps at least originally were expressions of religious sentiments, which lately have become profaned as we learn to treat nature rather perfunctorily. All arts, then, from this point of view, are sacred.

Now to the comparisons. All arts, I think, have the following things in common, and I shall attempt to give some examples from various cultures and specifically from Lakota culture:

1. All arts seek to *record* events that are deemed significant to the social group. Calendars are one obvious example of this important art form, one through which not only an important person, historical episode, or natural phenomenon is captured in a visual mode but through which also time itself is partly separated from profane time and made special.[11] The *waniyetu iyawapi*, or winter count, of the Lakota is, I think, a good example of calendrical art and compares favorably (from this structural-functional point of view) with other calendrical forms ranging from the printed calendars of contemporary times, all of which become highly individuated, to such ancient forms as the knotted ropes or calendrical *quipus* of the Inca.

2. All arts seek to *preserve* in the same way they seek to record. The two objectives are quite different even though they are quite compatible. Whereas recording is always particularistic, preservation may not be. For example, I have always been fascinated with the relief carvings of spiders,

turtles, and lizards on the stems of sacred pipes. Each one of these creatures means something to the old Lakota; the spider, for example, is a kind of cultural symbol sine qua non, a representation of the beginning of humanity and the recognition of just how frail humanity is. The turtle and lizard, similarly, are good-luck omens because the former is self-contained in his shell—that is, he lives in his own universe and can control it by ducking inside—while the latter is perceived to be blessed with long life. The turtle also looks, I think, a bit like the domoidal sweat lodge, itself a model of the universe within which the sun travels and the Four Winds govern during their respective seasons. All these simple representations carved into ashwood are highly symbolic and, to borrow a term from linguistics, polysemic—capable of expressing many meanings at the same time. The crucifix, or the American flag, for that matter, has this same capacity.

3. Next, I think that all arts seek to *duplicate* nature. The act of duplication is a political act; it permits the artist or artists to control nature. The nature of duplication has fascinated anthropologists for a great many years. The author of *The Golden Bough*, Sir James Frazer, neatly codified the notion of duplication when he wrote about laws of sympathetic magic; that is the law that states that *like produces like*.[12] Here I am reminded of various kinds of utensils, weapons, and badges of office found among the Lakota in which lightning is depicted. This usually means that if the owner of the object is not faithful to the responsibilities entrusted to him he will meet with a most terrible fate; namely, he will be struck by lightning. The rattle, too, is a form very much associated with lightning by the simple reasoning that the sound of the rattle is likened to the sound of thunder, which, of course, accompanies lightning. So the duplication of the visual image, that of lightning, is structurally related to the sound image of thunder, and both different kinds of artistic forms, one more graphic and the other more sculptural, duplicate nature in different but related ways. These analogies could be extended to include such diverse objects as the birds' nests made from sage that serve as containers for the rattles during the Yuwipi, to the crosspiece

Pipe carvers at the Senior Citizen Workshop, Pine Ridge, 1980.

of cherry wood in the sacred Sun Dance pole, both of which represent the nest of the Thunderbird. Realism in Western art is an expression of duplication and, I think, serves this same function.

4. Art seeks to *codify* the sentiments of a group of people— a nation or a tribe. Art comes to symbolize that group. Today, although this is a recent phenomenon, the star quilt becomes synonymous with the Lakota even though its techniques, forms, and colors were originally from the Amish and Mennonite people of Pennsylvania. Beadwork designs with a strong emphasis on a limited number of designs and colors serve the same function. So does the sacred pipe. What is important here is that art—even art forms from other cultures— can be manipulated to meet the needs of a single society.

5. Art seeks to *express* the sentiments of an individual. Here I want to emphasize that much of what actually is regarded as

High Eagle, Pine Ridge, South Dakota. Photograph taken September 14, 1945. High Eagle is dressed in the typical, beaded "chief's suit" of the period. Note the decorated pipe and pipe bag in his left hand. Courtesy U.S. Department of the Interior Library.

art or much that passes for art, as we say, can never be totally individualistic. All art must exist in a relevant context—a relevant cultural context—or it will not make sense; that is, it will not be art. But individuals, working within the relevance of their respective cultures, create; groups do not. This need for the individual to create, something that we might liken to inspiration, permits the individual's imagination to generate not so much new forms as variations of old ones. If we look at the form of design (as opposed to color), we see a natural continuity or structural relationship between hide painting, porcupine quillwork, beadwork, and ribbon or quilting work. We see among individual craftsmen a pride in their creations that somehow are capable of straddling a recognizable tradition on the one hand and a variation of that tradition, which is like no others, on the other. In fact, with the exception of the crassly created work for mass consumption, which is not an art form by anyone's definition, the artist is not permitted to copy; and in our society, we even have laws to prevent such artistic plagiarism.

6. Art seeks to *exaggerate*, particularly to magnify, extend, or expand—somehow enlarge—the common, the profane, the everyday occurrence. Art has the capacity, if not the duty, to represent ordinary events in heroic proportions. In this kind of translation, there is no chance for ambiguity—a common man or woman is somehow transformed through the magic of a visual halo in the Christian church. What the great religious people of all times are known for (and these are the subjects of painting and sculpture) are not their common everyday experiences but the multitudes of miracles attributed to them. The sacred White Buffalo Calf Woman, like the Virgin Mary, is made special by the attribution to her in art and mythology of a distinct quality serparating her unequivocally from common woman. The Virgin Mary is attributed with a virgin birth,[13] while the White Buffalo Calf Woman transforms herself into four different-colored buffalo calves before she departs from the Lakota village after having brought to the people the seven sacred rites. And the mighty spirits of the

dead who come to frighten the young man on a vision quest
wear black hoods and ride giant horses. They, in fact, are
giants themselves and lead before them their slaves, those
who have been struck by lightning because they could not live
up to their social responsibilities. These are the roots of heroic
art, the need to exaggerate that is common to all sacred art.

7. Conversely—and we should not be surprised by the next
type of comparison—art seeks to *underplay*, to *deemphasize*, to
diminish, to somehow reduce extraordinary phenomena so
that they may become humanly manageable. Art takes things
down to bite-size, if you will, so that their normally heroic
proportions will not intimidate the true believer. The great-
ness that is perceived to be untouchable by common man is
reduced so that it can be understood. Religious medals, crucifixes, and statues are made small so that they can be picked
up, handled, fondled, seen in all three dimensions, and examined closely. Growing Indian boys and girls are exposed to
countless art forms depicting human concerns: dolls, miniature tipis, small bone horses, and so on. All such items may
be easily controlled, thus allowing them to try their hand at
the vagaries of adulthood while they are still young. As they
grow older, they find that the spirits that control the universe
often take the form of small people and animals (like those
who live around springs and swamps) whose wooden forms
are often seen stashed away in trees, i.e., the *canotila*. Even
the sweat lodge and the sacred pipe are miniature representations of the entire universe, the first into whose bosom
one can crawl to explore, the latter whose properties may be
picked up and held in the hands.[14]

8. Finally, art seeks to *explain reality* by using contrasts; it
simplifies the complex and complicates the simple. The colors
black, red, white, and yellow simply stand (and here I am ex-
aggerating and understating) for the four directions, the four
seasons, and the animals and birds that represent those directions. Four basic colors are transformed into a complicated
message about the sacred Lakota universe. On the other hand,
the trim on a shirt or dress, whether rendered in beads or
quillwork, turns a simple straight line into an incredible host

of geometric and realistic boxes, circles, diamonds, triangles, and combinations of all of them—and all of this *without* any symbolic meaning.

From an anthropological perspective—which in my case seeks to examine visual representations from a structural and functional vantage rather than one based exclusively on false notions about materials and increased technological efficiency and concommitantly useless notions derived from the Western concept of progress—we can say that all arts of the world may be brought together under a universal banner if we accept that the way art functions is largely to record, preserve, duplicate, codify, express, magnify, deemphasize, and contrast—all functions to transforming, in culturally meaningful ways, nature into culture.

I should like to say also that art and religion are inseparable because both invoke in human beings the same kind of emotional response. Perhaps to talk about sacred art is redundant, although I suppose all of us understand what the terms mean and have been accustomed to seeing these terms juxtaposed.

Finally, one may call upon art historians and philosophers to give some thought to a structural and functional approach to the definition and classification of all arts. In the past, these disciplines have been greatly influenced by Western intellectual traditions. Even a cursory glimpse of the fifteen-volume *Encyclopedia of World Art*[15] reveals that American Indian art does not achieve the status afforded to most other art of the world except under the expected headings of magic, primitivism, and shamanism.[16] It is unlikely that a new classification system, one that does not distinguish between Art writ large and arts written with a small *a* and pluralized, will come into effect in a very short time, because we are all fortunately or unfortunately products of our own cultures and the values associated with them. Perhaps someday we may see art as no more and no less than the culturation of nature and, in that, a sacred form of expression, one in which, as Leonardo Da Vinci said, "nothing is wanting and nothing is superfluous."

CHAPTER 5

DUAL RELIGIOUS PARTICIPATION: STRATAGEMS OF CONVERSION AMONG THE LAKOTA

SIMULTANEOUS participation in two discrete religious systems is a widespread phenomenon found in those parts of the world where native peoples have been subjected to colonization and missionary influence.[1] I have restricted myself to the United States, where perhaps the most concrete examples are found among American Indian tribes, some of whose members belong to Christian denominations and at the same time regularly participate in traditional rituals.[2] Despite the ubiquity of dual religious participation, it has not been properly explained in anthropological literature. My own explanation will focus on the Oglalas of the Pine Ridge Indian Reservation in South Dakota.

Part of this analytical paucity derives from what Geertz has called an absence of "theoretical advances of major importance" in the anthropological study of religion (Geertz, 1966: 1). According to Geertz, most ideas about religion derive from Durkheim, Weber, Freud, and Malinowski, with only marginal modifications or expansions of ethnographic data. Anthropologists, he contends, have failed to look elsewhere, to philosophy, history, law, or the hard sciences, as these men did.

Equally prohibitive in finding new methods to explain religious phenomena is a preoccupation with our own cultural biases derived partly from the ideas of these contributors whom we continue to emulate. Leach has aptly pointed out that "anthropological theories often tell us more about the anthropologists than about their subject matter" (Leach 1969,

109; original, 1966). Perhaps this is nowhere more evident than in the anthropological studies of religion.

In the past, structural-functional models and psychological models have provided some insight with respect to how religious systems function as both statements of the social order and statements about how people feel about their religion (Leach 1958). But these kinds of models alone do not permit us to place a religious institution or system, however defined, in proper perspective once discrete cultural systems have come in contact with one another. Our willingness to note participation in more than one religious system as a by-product of culture contact, and then to be puzzled by it, is predicated further on unconscious, ethnocentric biases firmly rooted in the catholic dictum that, just as God is victorious over Satan, Christianity likewise conquers paganism. Anthropologists often have been chained by Christianity to preconceived notions about the ultimate and inevitable assimilation of American Indian belief systems. Thus we are predisposed to accept without challenge such statements as, "Syncretism . . . is a feature of virtually all contemporary Sioux religious practices" (Zimmerly 1969, 50). Or, "It was a great many years . . . before *the majority of Pine Ridge Indians became Christians,* in spite of the suppression of most of their native religious ceremonies" (Macgregor 1946, 91-92; italics added). Or perhaps, more audacious (since it appears in the *Pine Ridge Research Bulletin*), we learn that

> because of the fervor of early missionaries in attempting to stamp out "heathen" practices, the Sioux, at least initially, did not wholeheartedly embrace Christianity. Also, the missionaries' inflexibility in regard to Indian religion impeded the incorporation of native elements into Christian doctrine and rituals. One thus does not have, as in Roman Catholicism in many Indian cultures in Latin America, a syncretism of Christian and native practices within the well-established Christian churches. [Maynard and Twiss 1969, 1]

The authors of this statement are quick to direct us to a footnote on the same page that reads, "This is now being *remedied* somewhat" (italics added), and we are referred to an article in the same journal whose objective is to suggest that "one starting point in the blending of traditional Sioux Religion and the Christian Religion would be to transform the Sacred Pipe into a Christian prayer instrument" (Steinmetz 1969).[3]

Perhaps the alacrity with which anthropological investigators find the Lakota predestined to adopt Christianity as a belief system is predicated on the historical association of missionaries and anthropologists, for it is often difficult to discover empirical evidence for such religious transformations or substitutions. We often confuse public and private symbols, the former dealing with how people really interact with others, and the latter with how people feel about these interactions. Some anthropologists and religionists are more skeptical, however. Even Macgregor notes that "their acceptance of Christianity was at first, and continues to be to some extent today, an acceptance of the deity of their conquerors and a search for his power, without complete abandonment of the old beliefs" (Macgregor 1946, 92). Ruby states that many Lakota belong to Christian denominations but that few take these new religions seriously enough to abandon old beliefs (Ruby 1955, 16). Wissler, one of the prime skeptics, notes that Indians could understand the presence of numerous Christian denominations on the reservation, for they had many religious cults, but could not understand the "fanatical notion that a person could belong to but one of them at a time" (Wissler 1971, 155; original, 1938).[4]

There is an argument of sorts between the advocates of syncretism and the skeptics: they are dealing with seemingly unresolvable data. Thus dual religious participation has perplexed anthropologists, missionaries, and government bureaucrats for decades perhaps because the phenomenon appears to be a contradiction in terms. Most of the proselytizing religions of the world leave no room for ambiguity. Ideally, sectarian membership requires allegiance to specific deities and doctrines; false gods are eschewed. Sectarian rules do not restrict members to choosing only guardian spirits and patron saints, but they do dictate the parameters of social obligations and restrictions. Finally, if one discrete religious system, such as Roman Catholicism, defines itself, at least partly, in terms that explicitly forbid participation in another religion, what motivates people to participate in two such mutually self-excluding religious systems? What is their justification?

So far the attempt to unravel this paradox has been found in the interpretations of religious systems by their respective proponents. I am of the opinion that culture-boundedness and ethnocentrism alone marked the assimilative doom of Native American religions. Since Christianity was perceived to collide with native religion, missionaries interpreted the results in terms of conversion. Antiquarians "verified" these putative conversions by underscoring native religious practices as archaic vestiges of ritual and belief. Historians "documented" the interpretations of missionaries and antiquarians. And anthropologists "explained" these phenomena by turning to acculturation studies, a theoretical and methodological approach appropriate for analyzing technological change but deficient for the analysis of symbolic systems. Absent from the plethora of interpretations offered to explain the presence of dual religious organization were interpretations by Native Americans themselves, with the notable exception of those who professed membership in Christian sects (Macgregor 1946, Zimmerly 1969).

Acculturation was unconsciously treated as a one-way street, the subordinate society receiving new cultural goods from the dominant, but rarely or never reciprocating. Thus native religion was preordained to become dangerously susceptible to the overwhelming influences of Christianity, and Christianity was perceived to be impervious to external influence. But these perplexities and paradoxes were not based on empirical evidence. Rather, the rubrics of acculturation, missionization, and bureaucratization placed restrictions or limitations on the religious field that anthropologists were obliged to study.

It was essentially this limitation of field that prevented anthropologists from explaining dual religious participation on the basis of observable data. Only by eliminating our histori-

cal ethnocentrism and our predisposition toward interpreting
other interpretations can we arrive at new paradigms that will
beg new questions and answers. Rather than simply record
what we observe, or accept uncritically what others tell us, we
must look for meaning in each level of our investigation, historical, social, or cultural. At the beginning, we should look
for meaning in the social fact that at Pine Ridge individuals
and entire communities attend Catholic Mass or Episcopal
Communion on Sundays and spend other days of the week
attending to the sacred duties of the Sun Dance, the vision
quest, and the sweat lodge. Given what we understand about
both religious systems, how can this be reconciled? Even
more seemingly hypocritical, by Christian standards, how
can the medicine men who conduct native rituals join their
own adepts at the Communion rail, receiving sacramental
bread and wine from their Christian counterparts with whom
we presume them to be in competition? Furthermore, how do
we account for the fact that native peoples themselves, once
the subjects of proselytization, often become the proselytizers
of new religious systems antithetical to the old?

It has been convenient if not expedient in the past to answer these questions by stating that these are manifestations
of cultural adaptation. What we are witnessing here, some
will say, is a transitory stage that will lead eventually to the
total subsumation of native religion by Christianity. This can
be "demonstrated" by observing other kinds of data. For example, if an Indian shaman should carry a crucifix to the top
of a sacred butte for the purpose of warding off evil spirits, we
are quick to reduce this aspect of dual religious organization
to "syncretism." Or if sacred tobacco pouches are strung together so that they resemble a "rosary" and are called such by
the native, again we are, by force of habit, disposed to note its
"syncretic features." Syncretism is a concept so abstract that it
is almost useless as an analytical distinction. Yet despite its
inutility, syncretism has been conjured up to explain perceived change in native religion with respect to Christianity.
Thus Zimmerly attributes the contemporary native religious
philosophy of an Oglala medicine man to the profound influ-

ence of his early *Roman Catholic* training (Zimmerly 1969, 50; italics added).

We are not willing however, to apply the term "syncretism," whether analytically useful or not, to a religious ritual in which a Catholic priest offers up a sacred pipe (as Steinmetz has suggested) before mass, wearing vestments decorated in beads and quills. Historically and traditionally we would tend to interpret this use of native materials by a Catholic priest as strategy designed to win converts through a kind of moral deception, one deemed acceptable because the stratagem would ultimately lead to a civilized revelation rather than a primitive vision. But would we ever be willing to admit that the priest believed in the efficacy of the pipe? Were the trappings of native religion now part of his religious system? Was Christianity now beginning to exhibit the "syncretic" features of a pagan religion? Historically, we must answer no. While Christianity has been permitted to filter into native religion, evidenced in sacred material such as crucifixes and rosaries, native religion has not been permitted to infiltrate Christian belief. We would agree, I think, to accept the priestly overtures as a stratagem of the Catholic church, which, in the words of the Jesuits, "uses the best of any culture for its own advantage" (Holy Rosary Mission 1963, 20).

But to return to our initial problem of explaining dual religious participation, if we eliminate the convention of one-sided acculturation theories and ethnocentric biases, how do we explain the tendency of native peoples to participate in two discrete religious systems? Do they in fact "adore" two gods, one represented in the ritual paraphernalia of the Grandfathers, the other in the beaded chasuble, maniple, and stole of the priest? Are there in fact two separate sets of pantheons, cosmologies, and cosmogonies? Are the adepts, participants, or members living a religiously dualistic life; or do, in fact, the two religious systems represent for them two systems of quite different orders? If so, do they function in different capacities, and how are their structures related?

Here we meet head-on with one of the fundamental problems in explaining dual religious participation. Harking back to Geertz's appraisal of religious studies, we must recognize that, in the past, so-called explanations of native religion have been couched in religious terms. That is to say, religious *rituals* of one society have been used to explain the religious *beliefs* of another without an understanding of the extent to which the notion of "belief" among, say, Native Americans corrresponds with our own.[5] As we well know, to explain a phenomenon in terms of itself is to offer no explanation at all. Yet in the past, some have done precisely that. We expect Christianity and native religion to fulfill the same needs rather than disparate ones, and so we proceed to invent paradoxes that are the product of our minds, not the natives'. At the point of cultural contact, we anticipate a priori that the belief system of one society will collide with the belief system of another and produce either tension or conflation. Both systems will vie for the attention of the subordinate society, and eventually the native will believe in one or the other. But, of course, given these predispositions, the individual cannot believe in both. I agree that indeed he cannot believe in two religions, but this is not to say that he cannot participate in more than one.

It is useful for the moment to return to the structural-functional model of society that regards religion, economics, politics, and sociality as systems or aspects of social organization. Deloria has pointed out that the religion of a Native American society is often synonymous with its ethnic identity (a point that I have discussed also at length elsewhere [Deloria 1973; Powers 1977]). As such, religion serves as the essential integrative system of native society. We may, for the time being, think of both American Indian tribes and Euro-American society as separate functional systems that have come into contact. Inherent in any structural-functional model is its preoccupation with the notion of continuity in society, or, at the cultural level, the persistence of values. Once these societies have come in contact, we anthropologists are often prone to abdicate the functional model and switch to an acculturation model in an attempt to look at the diachronic relationship between two societies. Thus it is anticipated that the social, political, economic, and religious institutions or systems of the dominant society will, in fact, consume or subsume the respective social, political, economic, and religious institutions or systems of the subordinate society. In the process, traditional social organization is expected to give way to the organizing principles of the dominant society. Traditional political organization is replaced by bureaucracy. Subsistence economy is transformed into a market economy. And paganism succumbs to Christianity.

It is out of this presumed substitution of two systems of the same order that syncretism, as the term has been used historically, emerges. But as we have seen from some of the statements above, Christianity and native religion often are seen to coexist rather than conflate. It is not an either/or proposition; rather, Native Americans participate in them simultaneously. My own explanation for this phenomenon requires the retention of structural-functional models that view a society as a system and view sociality, politics, economics, and religion as aspects of this system. To structural-functional models I add historical depth, which gives me some indication of when and under what circumstances transformations of systems actually occur when cultures collide. Although my approach is sociological, I also employ historical and ethnohistorical data that serve as cross-checks for structural transformations. Metaphorically, I am giving Lévi-Strauss's notion of *bricolage*, the logical rearrangements of components of a system, a chronological frame. History may, in fact, be "history-for" (Lévi-Strauss 1966)—that is, viewed within a narrow perspective. But this makes it no less useful for understanding societies once their history has been written.

Before turning to dual religious participation at Pine Ridge, I first want to emphasize that religion in all societies is largely in the purview of ritual specialists. Most people in a society are not preoccupied with ritual; they are neither hyperreligious nor areligious but rather fall into the mid-range of a continuum. Secondly, I maintain that indeed there are Oglala who have converted to Christianity or who, through missionary education, have been brought up as Christians. Similarly, I maintain that there are many non-Christian Oglala who do not necessarily profess a belief in native religion. I am concerned primarily with those Oglala who actually participate simultaneously in two religious systems and how this seeming paradox can be explained profitably through sociological and historical analysis. Toward this goal I will argue that Christianity and Oglala religion coexist because they serve quite disparate functions. Oglala religion may be regarded as a system that maintains a set of beliefs and rituals sanctioned by supraempirical beings and powers, epitomized in the concept of Wakantanka. Christianity, on the other hand, serves other purposes—of a social, political, and economic nature—the combined structures and functions of which, along with native religion, guarantee the persistence of values underlying Oglala social and cultural identity.

I regard the participation by Oglala in Christian sects as social, political, economic, and religious strategies. Religious strategy in particular explains the participation of medicine men in Christian rituals for the purpose of understanding the supraempirical beings and powers of the white man.

I will focus on dual religious participation at Pine Ridge, South Dakota, beginning with the establishment of the reservation.

MISSIONARIES AT PINE RIDGE

Pine Ridge is situated in south-central South Dakota and is the home of 20,000 Oglala, the largest of the seven Teton divisions. The present reservation was established as a result of the Treaty of Fort Laramie in 1868 (although Pine Ridge did not become the agency until 1878) and today is the second-largest reservation in the United States. According to Utley: "The few Christian missionaries who labored among the Tetons since the 1840s had made almost no headway. In 1880 the political, social, and religious structure of the Teton Sioux remained largely intact" (Utley 1963, 21).

It would not be placing historical events entirely out of context to say that the missionaries have been on the Pine Ridge reservation as long as the Oglala have. The reservation, like others, began as a piece of political architecture designed to contain the Oglala so that the Anglo world around them could continue to progress at its present rate without interference; meanwhile the Oglala could be given the opportunity to catch up to "civilization." The infrastructure of the reservation contained the military and the missionaries whose responsibility it was to denativize the Oglala.

During the early reservation period, the Indian Bureau had assigned one denomination to each of the Sioux agencies. When Valentine T. McGillycuddy was agent at Pine Ridge, the Episcopalians made the most headway. They had established a mission at least by 1875 and, under the leadership of Bishop W. H. Hare, had maintained a monopoly over the Oglala (Maynard and Twiss, 1969:2).

In 1879, a Benedictine priest, the Reverend Meinrad McCarthy, arrived at Pine Ridge to establish a Roman Catholic mission and was promptly told to leave. It was not until McGillycuddy was succeeded by H. D. Gallagher, an Irish Catholic, that the Catholics were permitted to evangelize (Olson 1965, 308). With monies donated by Mrs. Catherine Drexel, of Philadelphia, a Catholic mission was built four miles north of Pine Ridge Agency and by 1888 was opened under the auspices of German Jesuits. The name was later changed from Drexel Mission to Holy Rosary Mission.[6]

The Roman Catholics at the mission, who traced their spiritual genealogy to Father De Smet, argued during the intervening decade that they were entitled to give further instructions to those Lakota who had already been baptized. The monopoly of the Episcopalians resulted in heated arguments among the members of the clergy, administrators, and eventually the Oglala themselves. The Catholics maintained that they were being discriminated against and that most of the Oglala would choose Roman Catholicism if given the chance (see particularly Goll 1940, 22–23).

Other denominations were also represented early in the reservation period, particularly the Presbyterians and the Congregationalists. Although many of the Oglala institutions were intact, increasing pressures on the Oglala during the period 1876–90 to take up the white man's road led many of the Indians into the various denominations. Macgregor has aptly pointed out that Christianity was the one part of the white man's life in which the Indian was accepted as equal (Macgregor, 1946:92), and it cannot be overemphasized that the Oglala have always maintained that the missionaries are basically good people. According to Utley:

> Even though they forever criticized good old Indian ways, the missionaries were kind, and the Sioux liked most of them well enough to attend services. They could not help noting with some confusion the different ways in which missionaries of different sects urged them to worship the same god, and all the ill-concealed hostility that the various sects often displayed toward one another. [Utley 1963, 33]

The conflict among denominations is a point to which I shall return.

Ben Black Elk, son and interpreter of Nickolas Black Elk, in a promotional photo. The words on the altar cloth translate "Holy, Holy, Holy." Courtesy Heritage Center, Inc.

The Indian chapel at Springcreek, on the Rosebud Reservation. Courtesy Heritage Center, Inc.

Once missionaries were established on the reservation, more came, and more land was obtained to expand each denomination's activities on the reservation (Deloria 1969, 101 passim). The building of the Catholic mission and chapels is well documented. Between 1893 and 1958, thirty churches were built in the Pine Ridge districts to serve Indians living on approximately 5,000 square miles of the reservation (Holy Rosary Mission 1963, 12–19). In 1969, it was reported by the Reverend William Fay, rector of the Holy Cross Episcopal Church in Pine Ridge, that the Episcopalians had twenty-eight churches on the reservation. [7] Since the coming of the Episcopalians, Catholics, Presbyterians, and Congregationalists, these denominations have been joined by the Body of

Christ, the Church of Latter-Day Saints, the Seventh-Day Adventists, the Church of God, Lutherans, the Gospel Missionary Union, the Methodists, the Baptists, and the Native American Church.

Most Christian Oglala belong to the Roman Catholic or Episcopal church (Maynard and Twiss 1969, 5–6), and I shall confine my remarks to these two, recognizing that similar relationships exist between the Oglala and the other denominations.

Part of the reason the Oglala "turned" to Christianity has by convention been described as evolving from two major factors. One is that the missionaries exercised their influence in having the federal government prohibit native religious ceremonies such as the Sun Dance and the Ghost-keeping Ceremony (Macgregor 1946; Brown 1953). Owing to the nature of reservation life, particularly the discontinuation of hunting and warfare, other rituals such as the sweat lodge, the vision quest, and puberty ceremonies allegedly became dysfunctional. The second factor, partly contingent on the first, is that many aspects of Christianity such as asceticism, the torture of the Crucifixion, giving away to others, and virginity "were not unconnected [in] Dakota beliefs and cultural values" (Macgregor 1946, 92).

As for the first point, it is a matter of historical record that the Sun Dance was banned from 1881 until 1933. But there is no evidence that the prohibition was acknowledged by the Oglala, and most contemporary medicine men maintain that the dance was practiced privately throughout the period of prohibition. [8] The other ceremonies continued without interruption and are still active. Second, the argument that Christianity had many features that were similar to native religion, thus making it enticing, does not obtain logically. If, in fact, the two religions exhibited similar characteristics (asceticism, torture, etc.), there is no logical reason why the Oglala should favor a Christian brand of religion over their own.

It is much more reasonable to assume that the Oglala became at least nominal members of Christian churches because the latter provided a kind of sanctuary from that part of the white world that regarded them as savage and hostile. If

Oglala native religion continued to persist through the early reservation period, despite the prohibitions imposed on the people by the missionaries and the government (and we still witness native religion today), it is illuminating to reconstruct the early reservation history in an attempt to see what precisely the Christian churches were doing for the Oglala. If, as Deloria states, tribal society is often synonymous with religious society, then perhaps it is useful to look at the way Christianity might aid the Oglala in organizing the social, political, and economic aspects of their society that were being carved away by the federal government. What we may find are not simple conflations and substitutions but structural transformations occurring in which the function of Christianity was to accommodate the now-dysfunctional aspects of Oglala society. In other words, Oglala social, political, and economic institutions of an earlier period persisted because they could express themselves through the organization of Christian churches, particularly through the relationships *between* those numerous denominations whose religious leaders often contradicted each other.

I am not willing to call these transformations simply manifestations of logical continuity. Rather, I argue that they were conscious stratagems employed at a time when the Oglala were struggling against all odds for mere survival. Here, of course, Lévi-Strauss's idea of *bricolage* is illuminating. Just as we see the myth-making handyman rearranging finite constructions and destructions of mythical ideas (Lévi-Strauss 1966), we see the structures of an earlier Oglala society being rearranged to conform to a new way of life imposed by the white man. But in the process of the transformation, old values persisted. The structure of Oglala society remained relatively constant because Christianity provided the right kind of organizing principle within which the Oglala could subsume native ideology. The way in which earlier forms of Oglala social, political, and economic behavior manifested itself, of course, changed: these behaviors could be expressed through membership in Christian denominations. But the structure of these institutions remained intact, the strongest being the re-

Catechist Silas Fills the Pipe. Courtesy Heritage Center, Inc.

ligious system that had not changed effectively even after the missionaries had begun to "convert" new believers. Thus the Oglala were not so much to become Christianized as Christianity was to become nativized.

To return to the idea that Christianity was used as a stratagem, how might it serve to replicate structurally the older institutions of prereservation Oglala society? Much of the evidence comes from missionary literature itself, which we could, of course, logically expect to be propagandistic. Contained in the sometimes detailed descriptions of early reservation life, however, once the propaganda has been stripped away, lies interesting data to support the notion that the Oglala in fact used Christianity consciously and positively in order to survive. In the process of surviving, many ideas of Oglala social structure remained intact. Using mainly Jesuit literature, I will now examine social, political, economic, and religious stratagems associated with Christianity.

SOCIAL STRATAGEMS

By social stratagems I mean those interactions between the Oglala and Christian denominations that somehow guarantee continuity in such institutions as kinship, marriage, and membership in the basic sociopolitical unit of the prereservation period, the *tiyošpaye* (cf. Feraca 1966; Powers 1977).

When the Oglala were first forced onto the reservation, they were organized into 7 *tiyošpayes*. *Tiyošpayes* largely regulated marriage and, to some extent, political authority. Leaders often quarreled with each other, with much fission and fusion resulting. Oglala were born into *tiyošpayes*, and exogamous principles dictated that one choose a spouse from outside one's own. After being moved into the reservation, each of the 7 *tiyošpayes* relocated on various parts of the reservation where they formed the nucleus of today's reservation communities. As the reservation population grew, the 7 primary *tiyošpayes* fissioned into 89, and today there are 50 communities (Maynard and Twiss 1970). Most members still recognize their affiliation with the original *tiyošpayes*.

After the establishment of Catholic and Episcopalian mission chapels in the local communities, the Oglala began to attend services. Macgregor points out:

> Individuals in the rural communities all tend to join one church, especially if there is any common bond *of a band origin*. It was noted that, in many families, a Catholic or Protestant has joined the church of the other upon marriage. In one family a Catholic mother became an Episcopalian, but her Episcopalian daughter became a Catholic upon her marriage. Children in one family may be divided in church membership between Catholic and Protestants without cónflict. [Macgregor 1946, 96–98; italics added][9]

If we were to read *tiyošpaye* for Catholic or Episcopalian denomination, we would see that marriage practices remained the same as those of an earlier period, but their cultural manifestation was now couched in terms of *church* membership. Thus marriage outside a denomination was analogous to marriage outside one's *tiyošpaye*. Interestingly, Macgregor misconstrues this new form of organization, believing that, "this stimulation of competition and exclusiveness in church groups, developed under white leadership among a single and once strongly integrated people, has been *injurious to social cohesion* and has brought confusion and criticism among the Indians" (Macgregor 1946, 98; italics added).

However, the idea of having children representing different denominations in the same household was not confusing to the Oglala. The denomination, like the *tiyošpaye*, made references to natal membership, not local residence. It would seem that the exclusiveness of church membership (or, rather, *tiyošpaye* membership) favored social cohesion for it mirrored the precise social structure of the Oglala before the coming of the missionaries. In particular, the hostility between Christian denominations was a structural analogue of the traditional hostility between *tiyošpaye* leaders.

The structural and functional similarities of the denomination and *tiyošpaye* become even clearer when we learn that "one of the chief sources of conflict particularly to the missionaries, was the unwillingness of the Indians to accept marriage as a religious rite" (Macgregor 1946, 93). Marriage the "Indian way" is still practiced on the Pine Ridge Reservation to the consternation of the missionaries who attempt to remarry persons in the various churches to make them bona fide in the eyes of God. Structurally and functionally, the institution of marriage has not changed.[10]

Christianity also provided an expression of social structure at another level of integration, namely, the institution of Christian convocations. The Catholic Congress was founded by Bishop Marty as a means of preventing "vicious revivals" of customs such as the giveaway. According to the Jesuit Goll, between 1900 and 1913, 3,000 persons attended these congresses. They were held alternately on all the Lakota reservations, and each year wagon loads of Lakota would travel to the host reservations.

Goll states that when the Indians traveled those days the whole family went by wagon. A caravan of forty or fifty made the journey. They stopped at places designated by certain officials, and families *from the same districts* were assigned camping grounds, in such a way that the assembly formed a large circle, and a formal welcome was made in a bower of branches (Goll 1940, 39–43). Thus, even in intergroup activities, the Oglala by camping along district lines essentially maintained the structural feature of camping along *tiyošpaye* lines.[11]

Macgregor points out that both the Episcopalians and the Catholics held summer conventions, stating that, although "no Indian ceremonial is a part of these meetings, the summer gathering of friends and relatives from different parts of the reservation and the camping in tents give the convocations some of the social function of the Sun dance" (Macgregor 1946, 97). My own understanding here is that the convocation allowed the Oglala an opportunity to exhibit the structural and functional features of a tribe—that is, an assemblage of *tiyošpayes*.

Thus one way we can explain Oglala participation in various Christian sects is on the basis of a stratagem designed to guarantee continuity to earlier forms of kinship, marriage,

and socially integrative processes that did not require belief in
the doctrines of the respective Christian sects. The marriage
practices of the Christians were often in fact antithetical to
what the Oglala perceived to be proper behavior. A Catholic
marrying a Catholic from the same district would be breaking
the rule of exogamy inherent in the *tiyošpaye* principle.

POLITICAL STRATAGEMS

By political stratagems I mean those interactions between the
Oglala and Christian sects that deal with concepts of power
and authority, decision-making processes, military interven-
tion, and imposition of a bureaucratic structure on the Oglala
people.

To turn again to the original *tiyošpayes*, each of them was
associated with certain political figures. Perhaps the best
known on the Pine Ridge Reservation are Red Cloud, who
headed the *tiyošpaye* known as the Bad Faces, and Little
Wound, who headed the Payabya. Red Cloud has been attributed with having demanded that the Catholics be permitted to
evangelize on the Pine Ridge Reservation, while Little Wound,
whose descendants still live in the vicinity of Kyle, South Dakota, was considered the strongest of Episcopalian supporters.

Red Cloud, of course, is more famous as the only Indian to
win a war with the federal government; it culminated in the
Treaty of Fort Laramie. A number of books have been writtten
about this controversial Oglala leader (see particularly Hyde
1956; Olson 1965). He is assessed as anything from the greatest warrior of the Sioux to the greatest charlatan for having
signed the treaty in the first place. Given either predisposition, he was unquestionably the most respected or feared Indian in the area before the establishment of the Pine Ridge
Reservation. I think it is fair to say that he was a man of vision
who recognized that the white man would eventually dominate and that measures should be taken to understand the
decision-making process followed in Washington. He was an
astute politician who believed that Indians should fight for
the rights that perhaps he had partly given away. My purpose

here is not to attack or defend Red Cloud but to indicate his position with respect to the presence of missionaries at Pine Ridge.

Red Cloud was the hero of the Jesuits. It is suggested that he met Father De Smet in 1851 and at that time was on the way to conversion to Catholicism.[12] Ironically, the hostility between the Episcopalians and the Catholics has always been regarded by the Jesuits as a denial of religious freedom to the Oglala. Red Cloud emerges as a champion of the Black Robes (as they are called, to distinguish them from the Episcopalian White Robes).[13] He is quoted as saying to Father Florentine Digman, a Jesuit who arrived from Saint Francis Mission, on the Rosebud, to serve at Holy Rosary Mission, "Already years ago I asked the Great Father for Blackrobes to be our teachers because they were the first ones who brought us the words of the Great Spirit" (Holy Rosary Mission n.d.).

The Jesuits point out that Red Cloud had argued for the Catholic mission to be established for a full 18 years before a change in agency administration allowed it to become a reality. But despite Red Cloud's support of the Black Robes, not all his motives were religious. According to historians, both Red Cloud and Spotted Tail had pleaded with President Rutherford B. Hayes at the White House in 1877 that "they wanted Catholic priests, the Blackrobes, *who would teach them how to read and write English*" (Olson 1965, 251–52; italics added). Hyde gives more details:

> Spotted Tail and his Chiefs were annoyed with the Episcopalians, who had had a missionary at the old agency as far back as 1875. The chief said that the White Robes had not taught one Sioux child to speak or to write English. As for the teaching of Christianity, that did not interest most of the chiefs. All they desired was to have some fullblood Sioux boys taught to read and write English, so that they might act as interpreters and also write letters from the chiefs to the officials in Washington. [Hyde 1956, 16–17][14]

The importance of having young Lakota who could read and write English cannot be underestimated. The Oglala were at the mercy of agency interpreters, and much of the hostility between *tiyošpaye* leaders has been attributed to faulty, if not specious, translation. The most famous incident, of course, although still disputed, is the assassination of Crazy Horse. Hyde believes that misinterpretation, in fact, had nothing to do with the murder of this Oglala leader; nevertheless, many Oglala believed that it did and wanted to take precautions.[15]

In addition to educating the Lakota, the missions served as political sanctuaries during the critical period 1878–90. Anyone who was even nominally a member of a Christian sect was less threatening to the white administration and, more important, less threatened. The missionaries stood not only for religious conversion but for freedom from political persecution. The only "good" Indian (since he could no longer be legally killed) was a Christian Indian.

ECONOMIC STRATAGEMS

By economic stratagems I mean the interactions between the Oglala and Christianity, which were predicated on rather basic needs: food, clothing, and shelter. A subsistence economy based on hunting was ended by whites, who intentionally killed off the buffalo. The Oglala were expected eventually to become farmers and ranchers but most never did, for several reasons. First, the exploitation of the land was antithetical to their belief system. Second, if they had chosen to become farmers or ranchers, it would have been virtually impossible to do so, since herds of cattle and implements were diverted from the Oglala and sold on the frontier black market by unscrupulous whites. Finally, most Oglala simply lacked any interest in farming and ranching.

Christian churches took over much of the economic function as part of their humanitarian offices. Not only did the agency become a distribution center (Pine Ridge village is called Wakpamni, meaning 'distribution' in Lakota), but so did the churches, in particular once annuities promised by treaty to the Oglala had been stolen, lost, or otherwise diverted from those for whom they were originally intended.

Being a member of a Christian denomination partly ensured mere economic survival for the Oglala. It was—and still is—common knowledge on the Pine Ridge Reservation that attendance at Sunday services greatly increased if meals were provided. When missionaries attempted to reduce food distribution, attendance decreased. One is mindful of Radcliffe-Brown's theory of the relationship between sickness and curing: people get sick *because* there are rituals to cure them. At Pine Ridge, the Oglala did not engage in Christian ritual, part of which included a feast. Rather, they engaged in Christian feasts, part of which included a ritual.

Ruby's statement that "church gives Indians a chance to congregate—they enjoy eating, and many depend on church for clothing" (Ruby, 1955: 16) cannot be taken too lightly. The Catholics, in particular, fed, clothed, and sheltered children as well as educated them. The Jesuits have thoroughly documented the use of food as an inducement to come to church or catechist services, and at least one devout Oglala catechist died penniless because he had expended all his earnings on providing feasts for people at worship services. One writer states: "Paul Catches made feasts for the Indians at St. Peter's in order to catch them. He became a poor man using this technique of conversion, but he died a good death in 1916" (Holy Rosary Mission 1963, 28). Furthermore, "many of the Catholics . . . were baptized at Manderson where they got their rations" (Holy Rosary Mission 1963, 16).[16]

At a procession in Oglala, South Dakota, during the feast of Corpus Christi in 1922, the local trader expressed some disbelief that so many Indians had come since no provisions were on hand. He said that it was "scarcely credible that so many Indians would come and take part without getting beef or bread" (Holy Rosary Mission 1963, 29).

Since the earliest establishment of the missions, churches have been distribution centers for clothing sent to the Indians mainly from good samaritans in the East. Holy Rosary Mission was perhaps the largest. Originally, needy Indians were simply invited to come to the Mission to select clothing for the entire family. In the early 1970s, I observed that the mission's

The Reverend Wilfred M. Mallon, S.J., from Holy Rosary Mission and William Spotted Crow, Sun Dance director, August, 1945. Courtesy Heritage Center, Inc.

Tom Yellow Bull teaching the catechism. Courtesy Heritage Center, Inc.

policy was changed somewhat. The fathers, in an attempt to "instill pride" in the Oglala, began charging nominal prices for clothing (twenty-five cents for a pair of shoes, etc.). The Oglala, knowing that the clothing was sent free to the mission, protested, saying that the missionaries were trying to exploit them.

The missionaries also gave meager financial assistance to church members. In addition to providing menial labor around churches, both Episcopalians and Catholics maintained lay readers or lay catechists who preached in the absence of priests. Pine Ridge has never been adequately staffed by clergy, given the size of the Indian population and the difficulty of traveling across the reservation to remote communities. Thus the services of clergy were augmented by layreaders among the Episcopalians, and catechists among the Catholics. The catechists received ten dollars a month for their services (Holy Rosary Mission 1963, 20).

It was noted by missionaries that Christian church members appeared to live in better houses, have better clothing,

The Episcopal Cemetery at Kyle, on the Pine Ridge Reservation.
Photograph by the author.

and better nutrition than non-Christians. This, of course, has
been translated to mean that Christians were, in fact, more
"civilized" than pagans. There is truth in the observation, of
course, but for different reasons. By belonging to a Christian
sect, an Oglala's chance of survival was improved through a
guarantee of the basic necessities of life, which was an essential business of the missionaries. It has been also noted that
Episcopalians reached more conservative full bloods. If we
turn to the community of Kyle, we find that it seems to function with less turmoil than other communities. But one might
equally posit that this is because the residents are conserva-
tives rather than because they are Episcopalians.

Finally, I believe that there is a direct relationship between
economic stratagems and decline in church membership,
which has little to do with belief. Many of the economic es-
sentials provided by the various denominations are being
taken over by government agencies through employment programs and welfare. These programs may account for the de-

cline in church membership better than nonempirical "evidence" such as loss of faith, or native religious "revitalization."

RELIGIOUS STRATAGEMS

One of the tasks of the missionary is literally to count his blessings. After seventy-five years of Christian service to the Oglala, the Jesuits reported their spiritual achievements in the following way:

> Since the founding of Holy Rosary Mission there are 13,712 recorded baptisms, 1,666 marriages and 1,441 funerals. Countless classes of religious instruction have been taught at the Mission and in the Government schools throughout the entire reservation. In addition to the many confessions, there were approximately 50,000 Holy Communions during this last school year. [Holy Rosary Mission 1963, 10]

Of course, caution must be exercised in attempting a statistical analysis of the figures for baptism, marriage, and funerals. Adequate population-distribution figures for the Oglala did not exist until recent years. Simply dividing the numbers for each of these church services by 75, however, we arrive at an annual average of 183 baptisms, 22 marriages, and 19 funerals ministered by the church each year since 1888. The total number of "Holy Communions" for the year does not tell us how many received "First Communion," which would be statistically interesting since there must be, according to church law, a correlation between "Baptism" and "First Communion." Despite the unavailability of these variables and others, it would appear that the church's record of conversion and other services is statistically negligible, particularly in view of the dramatic increase in Oglala population since the turn of the century. Any analysis is further complicated by the fact that Oglala tribal enrollment has never been completed, and there is currently a heated debate raging over "blood quantum" within the Oglala Sioux Tribal Council and its constituents. It is conceivable that those converted or otherwise ministered to by the church might not be regarded as "Indian" by those Oglala who are considered bona fide members of the tribe.

Also writing in 1963, Feraca noted that "religious concepts of the Teton Dakota of South Dakota are basically unchanged, and prereservation beliefs, practices and cults are by no means stagnant, but, in many cases are flourishing" (Feraca 1963, vii). The alleged "impact" of the church versus the persistence of native religion is best explained by the fact that "on the whole, most of the clergymen are quite unaware of the existence of many cults, and moreover would be surprised that any of them are active or vital in the life of the Teton. Church attendance, however, is poor and church marriages are becoming a rarity" (Feraca 1963, 8).

The intermittent waxing and waning of Christian influence is also a part of our ethnocentrism. We have no evidence for the "impact" of Christianity nor the "flourishing" of native beliefs. Historically, the Oglala trod between both kinds of religious participation depending on situational needs. Even the oldest and staunchest supporters of Christianity left the fold occasionally, particularly under pressure from the whites, and sometimes the Indians. During the Ghost Dance movement of 1888–90, precisely the period when the Jesuits were establishing Holy Rosary Mission: "Red Cloud, forgetting that he was a Roman Catholic, now stated that he believed in the messiah and that the people should begin the ghost dance. Other chiefs were of the same opinion, although most of them were Christian converts" (Hyde 1956, 242). Furthermore, "It was Little Wound, a notable progressive and supposedly a loyal Episcopalian, who led the Pine Ridge ghost dancers" (Hyde 1956, 250).

During the Ghost Dance, and after the Wounded Knee massacre, both Episcopalians and Catholics figured prominently. The Episcopal Church at Pine Ridge served as a field hospital for wounded Indians. The Catholics, particularly Father Jutz of Holy Rosary, risked his life to intercede between the government and the Ghost Dancers during the tense period after Wounded Knee. Within less than ten years after the massacre both denominations were employing Oglala as catechists and layreaders to help preach the word of the Christian god and to substitute as ministers when ordained priests were unable to visit the outlying communities. The Catholics formed the Saint Joseph and Saint Mary societies for the purposes of organized prayer. The leaders of these societies were called, respectively, "Grandfather" and "Grandmother" (terms also used appropriately to address *Oglala* religious leaders).

Interestingly enough, most of the catechists were native medicine men. Not only had they allegedly converted from paganism to Christianity, but they often converted to more than one Christian denomination at the same time.

In speaking of the turn of the century, the Jesuits mention a number of devout catechists. For example, Ivan Star was one with poor knowledge of English, but he was an "enemy of the Indian dances and was invited frequently *by Protestants* to pray in their homes" (Holy Rosary Mission 1963, 16; italics added). Similarly, Silas Fills the Pipe was an Episcopal layreader for twenty-five years before he became a Catholic catechist (Holy Rosary Mission 1963, 28). Perhaps the most famous of the catechists was Black Elk, who is described by the Jesuits as "a pagan medicine man converted by Fr. Lindebner in 1905. . . . Neibert's (*sic*) book, Black Elk Speaks, is a great injustice to him since it describes him as the pagan he no longer was" (Holy Rosary Mission 1963, 29).

The participation by Oglala religious leaders in Christian services has continued through the present. The reason for this conversion has been normally ascribed to the remarkable similarity between Christianity and native religion, which I have mentioned before. As Utley has stated: "Now confronted with unmistakable evidence of the power of the white man, they logically turned to the white man's God for this brand of power. But they did so without giving up the old gods" (Utley 1963, 34).[17]

Unquestionably, the Oglala believed that all power ultimately derived from supernatural sources. The white man's power was no different. The manifestations of such power— the horse, the gun, and alcohol—were appropriately regarded as *wakan*—sacred—by the Oglala when first they came in contact with them. Thus the religious leaders participated in the Christian denominations, not only for social, political, and economic purposes but because they were curious about the source of the white man's power, the white man's god. By understanding the source of this power, the Oglala might be in a better position to coexist with the white man. Perhaps some could even learn how to control the white man's god and in so doing control the white man.

The missionaries were unaware that native Oglala religious leaders were not only ritual practitioners but also philosophers. As philosophers, the medicine men argued, unnoticed by whites, among themselves and their adepts about the efficacy of the white man's god and the priests. The medicine man who sat in the front pew of church and received Holy Communion was there to observe the white man's gods and priests. He was there to see whether miracles happened and whether the priest misbehaved (after all, as some medicine men said, they preached against the use of alcohol but actually drank wine on Sundays during the rituals).

The Oglala who participated in both religious systems never for once doubted the power of the white man, but neither did they doubt the power of *Wakantanka*. As one man summed it up:

> I found that their [whites'] Wakan Tanka the superior . . . and have served Wakan Tanka according to the white people's manner and with all my power. I still have my *wašicun* (ceremonial pouch or bundle of a shaman) and I am afraid to offend it because the spirit of an Oglala may go to the spirit land of the Dakota. [Quoted in Macgregor 1946, 92]

This notion of a dual hereafter is still prevalent today.

Perhaps the native medicine men were astonished and their own belief system reinforced when, in the mid-1960s, many of the Christian denominations began interjecting Oglala ritual into their own. This, of course, was a stratagem of the church, but its interpretation by the Oglala ritual practitioner was that at least the Christians were beginning to see the light. Were they not praying with the pipe, the essential integrative symbol of Oglala religion? They decorated the church in a manner significant to Oglala people with proper color symbolism, the Thunderbird, and other Indian designs. They called their belief system Christianity, but surely it was becoming native Oglala religion.

At present, not only do the religious leaders of Christian denominations continue to inject native ritual into their own, but they increasingly are attending such native rituals as Yuwipi. Here they freely participate, even going so far as to offer up Christian prayers to what the Oglala believe to be native powers. The missionaries explain their participation as an attempt to reach out to the people and demonstrate their willingness to understand the belief system of their potential converts. But the Oglala religious leaders interpret this quite differently. The need for the priests to understand the supernatural world of the Oglala is no different from the Oglala priests' determination to understand the supernatural world of the whites. At the level of public ritual, the two religions conjoin; but at the level of private belief, Christianity and native religion, the respective components of dual religious participation at Pine Ridge, are separate and always have been.

My major point in the foregoing argument is that the phenomenon of dual religious participation, one that is pervasive throughout the world wherever large and small societies have come in contact, is best explained as a coexistence of two disparate religious systems. On the one hand, the native system satisfies needs we may call religious, in the sense that people require a belief in supraempirical beings and powers whom they call upon in culturally prescribed ways to address epistemological questions unanswerable by purely empirical means. On the other hand, the religious system of the dominant society—in the case of the Oglala, Christianity—represents a system that, with respect to native peoples, satisfies other kinds of exigencies, needs not normally associated with the supernatural, except perhaps marginally where the institutions of politics, economics, etc., may somehow be ascribed to a miraculous inception. Here the second, intrusive religious system provides an infrastructure upon which older, dysfunctional institutions may persist, clothed in the trappings of a new age but nonetheless significant to the Oglala. It is in the guise of Christianity and its interdenominational feudings that we find a structural replication of Oglala institutions now renderred defunct by the onslaught and conquest of the white man.

That the Oglala have taken to Christianity is largely a matter of our own faith, partly inspired by missionary predictions that the Oglala were doomed to assimilation into the Christian faiths. But as I have pointed out, empirical evidence has pointed to another kind of solution to the paradox. As a means of survival and adaptation to the unalterability of the white man's dominance, Christianity has been used in such a way that old cultural institutions and their associated values may persist under new labels. As I have shown, Christian denominations and the particular unamicable relationships between sects have served the Oglala strategically with regard to a number of social, economic, political, and religious ends. In so doing, they have maintained the structural integrity of their social organization through the transformation of dysfunctional institutions into functional ones.

To what extent my explanation of dual religious participation at Pine Ridge can serve as a model for cross-cultural comparison is contingent upon further research among other peoples of the world. Intuitively, I do not believe that Pine Ridge and the Oglala provide an example of a unique situation. Other examples, such as the Code of Handsome Lake among the Iroquois, exist. Perhaps the other religions that have been tentatively labeled "syncretic" may prove to exhibit the characteristics of logical transformations based on earlier cultural content. It is anticipated that reinterpreting religious groups or movements that have earned these particular labels will meet with some objection. Even among the Oglala, the position of the Native American Church or so-called Peyote Cult, is problematic. In distinguishing between syncretism as a category (which it is not) and a process (which it is), the Native American Church can only be regarded as a Christian sect, despite the prevalence of native ritual practices. But perhaps this Christian sect serves as a dialectic between Christianity and native religion, and only time will tell to what extent its influence will be felt in either Christian or native religious spheres.

Viewing American Indian societies from the perspective of cultural persistence rather than assimilation will require that we also reinterpret prior notions regarding revivalism and revitalization. Empirically we may state that there are more Oglala today participating in native religious ceremonies than, say, twenty-five years ago. But it would be far too simple to conclude that what we are witnessing is a resurgence in native religious interests. It would also be false to assume that the Oglala are "returning" to native belief because Christianity has "failed" them. These views, widely held by anthropologists and missionaries alike, tell us more about structural continuity and the persistence of values in non-Indian society than they do about the state of Native American religion.

CHAPTER 6

ALTERNATIVES TO WESTERN PSYCHOTHERAPY: THE MODERN-DAY MEDICINE MAN

We have learned that an individual in isolation from society is a psychological fiction.

Sapir (1966, 158)

In a delightful book on cross-cultural psychiatry *The Mind Game: Witchdoctors and Psychiatrists*, by E. Fuller Torrey, the author states: "If prostitution is the oldest profession, then psychotherapy must be the second oldest." He continues, saying that although the socioeconomic aspects of both have been well known for centuries, the "technical details of what actually transpires behind closed doors have been curiously relegated to the realm of whispers" (Torrey, 1972, 172).

In this context, I must regard myself as a member of perhaps the third-oldest profession, that of the professional snooper into the lives and customs of other people (including prostitutes and psychotherapists) who wishes to open those doors and investigate more closely the psychotherapeutic techniques of a non-Western people who have their own alternatives to Western psychotherapy.[1] The ritual specialists, or psychotherapists—since psychotherapy is essentially what they are best at doing—call themselves medicine men.

This chapter alternates between two major themes: (1) the historical and functional relationship between psychiatry and cultural anthropology, which in my opinion has not yet had the opportunity to reach florescence, and (2) the relationship between Western and non-Western—and in this instance American Indian—forms of psychotherapy with a glimpse of a psychotherapeutic ritual from a northern Plains tribe.

One of the things I want to stress is the similarity between Western and non-Western therapists. First, just as one is told to shop around for a good therapist in our own society, it is also considered wise to seek out a good medicine man in non-Western society. This has come about, I think, over the past five years or so because of the discovery that the psychotherapeutic process or ritual not only is controlled and manipulated by social factors but in fact stands as a symbol or metaphor of social change itself. The stated ability of any psychotherapist to treat or cure a patient is at the same time a statement about his ability to control those social factors that have in fact led to the illness. With American Indians (and I suspect that this would hold true with other societies that find themselves in a similar historical and structural relationship to a dominant, colonizing society) the problem of identifying social factors is that there are not one but two sets: (1) the social factors inherent in the Indian society and (2) those inherent in the dominant society. Thus, if the psychotherapeutic process is a statement about controlling social factors, the modern-day medicine man is moving increasingly toward control in two societies. Medicine men who at one time were satisfied with curing patients suffering from diseases believed to be a product of Indian society are now trying to cure illnesses presumed to have been brought to the Indians by Europeans. In shopping around, the Indian seeks in fact, a bargain—two psychotherapists for the price of one.

Still another similarity comes to mind (and there will be more). It is not only the Western psychotherapist who is vulnerable to malpractice suits. One summer an Indian man who was convinced (by the medicine man) that he should stick his arm in boiling water, a ritual perceived to have been common in the old days—for retrieving a choice part of cooked meat—decided that at the moment of truth, he had some misgivings. The medicine man, however, insisted and grabbed the man's arm, thrusting it in a pot of boiling water. The man received severe burns, ultimately leading to amputation of the hand and later decided to sue the zealous medicine man for malpractice. The therapy failed, but only because the medicine man was a quack. The belief system lives on. (Incidentally, the suit never came to court.)

There has been a long tradition in American anthropology according to which cultural anthropologists have joined with psychologists and psychiatrists in attempting to gain access to how American Indians think. This interest in fathoming the native's cognition has led to a long relationship between psychoanalysis and the interpretation of culture. In his influential book *Psychoanalysis and Culture*, Geza Roheim suggests that the methods employed by cultural anthropologists to analyze culture simply do not fit the facts and that psychoanalytical method as an interpretative tool explains more. His preference for the latter was based on what he perceived to be a richer understanding of universal symbols, such as the Oedipus complex, whose underlying significance was sometimes blurred by levels of context. The context, of course, was of the utmost importance to the cultural anthropologist who argued, in the manner of the Harvard scholar Clyde Kluckhohn, that if psychoanalysts were to make their own views acceptable to cultural anthropology they would have to consider their interpretations within the larger framework of the context of a given culture, a point of view that still exists today in the works of most cultural anthropologists.

According to Edward Sapir, who wrote extensively on transcultural psychiatry, psychoanalysts have welcomed studies in cultural anthropology because:

> The resemblances between the content of primitive ritual— and symbolic behavior generally among primitive peoples—and the apparently private rituals and symbolisms developed by those who have greater than normal difficulty in adjusting to their social environment are said to be so numerous and far-reaching that the latter must be looked upon as an inherited survival of more archaic types of thought and feeling. [Sapir 1966, 148–49]

On the other hand, the cultural anthropologist

is disposed to think that if the resemblances between the neurotic and primitive which have so often been pointed out are
more than fortuitous, it is not because of a cultural atavism
which the neurotic exemplifies but simply because all human
beings, whether primitive or sophisticated in the cultural sense,
are, at rock bottom, psychologically primitive, and there is no
reason why a significant unconscious symbolism which gives
substitutive satisfaction to the individual may not become so-
cialized on any level of human activity. [Sapir 1966, 149–50]

Here I do not want to enter the ongoing argument over the
relative merits or shortcomings of each disciplines' theories
and methodologies, particularly today when a strong case is
being made—in the spirit of scientific ecumenicism and sociobiology—that everybody who was once regarded as being
wrong is now right. This is a point Sapir perhaps wisely interpreted when he noted that "there is no mischief in all this,
once it is clearly understood that the scientist of man has chief
concern for science, not for man, and that all science, partly
for better and partly for worse, has the self-feeding voracity of
an obsessive ritual" (Sapir 1966, 102).

Here we may simply assume that cultural anthropology and
psychiatry have much in common; and as it has been noted
frequently, the shaman—or however called: witch doctor, sorcerer, magician, conjurer, etc.—probably has a frequency of
cures in his society equal to the psychotherapist in his own.

What has not been taken into consideration yet, I think, is
that today many people—perhaps more of them clients of anthropologists than of psychotherapists—live essentially between two or even more cultures. Each culture has its own
language, its own social and economic propensities, its own
form of local politics, its separate and often unequal kinship
systems, its own expressive culture in music, dance, poetry,
and (perhaps most relevant here) its own religious system
and somewhere subsumed within that, its own system of diagnosing and curing what is perceived to be somatic and psychosomatic illness.

People are often swept up by two cultures whose value systems are dramatically opposed to each other. When this hap-

pens, the shaman not only provides an alternative form of healing to his patients but in fact may stand in opposition to the Western psychotherapist. In some cases, this relationship may be harmless if not amicable. In others, however, one of which I shall discuss further along, the modern-day medicine man may see the role of the Western psychotherapist as antagonistic and threatening to his own, in effect provoking more harm in his patients than help. All of this has come about, I think, as a result of the reservation system, and I shall explain later what I mean.

I should like to say a few words about the role of this modern-day medicine man, especially as the role applies to North American Indians and specifically to the ritual practitioners on the Pine Ridge Reservation.

I am first struck by the terms employed to identify him— take *shaman*, a word from the Tungus tribe of Siberia meaning "to cry out," a term that has been adopted by anthropologists, historians of religion, sociologists, and psychologists to refer to a person, usually but not always male, who cures patients of what we would term psychosomatic illness by so-called supernatural means.

The continuous use of exotic words such as shaman, I think, tends to establish and maintain a superficial distance between ritual practitioners, or healers if you will, who for all practical purposes are functional equivalents. Hence the shaman as healer is at once suspect to Western traditional medicine and psychotherapy partly because the very nomenclature employed to classify him is seen to be somewhat exotic, suggesting his inferiority to the psychotherapist. We imply a primitive form of healing by naming it with a primitive term.

The second thing that strikes me about the concept of the primitive healer is the enormous literature, which has as a serious point of agreement the fact that the shaman is seen, at least by cultural anthropologists who express interest in culture and personality studies, as exhibiting in *himself* the characteristics of mental illness, to wit, schizophrenia. We seem to be at a second disadvantage in our attempts to understand the efficacy of the modern-day medicine man when we contrast him with our own psychotherapists. What emerges is a comparison of a rather prejudicial sort, I think, one wherein Western society patients perceived to be potentially ill are treated by doctors perceived to be sane, while in Indian society, at least according to the social scientists, patients perceived to be potentially sane are treated by doctors perceived to be ill.

Perhaps the rate of psychosis among shamans compared to that among Western therapists is analogous to their respective rates of cure. Those rates are seen to be equal, or approximately so, even though I am not aware of any studies that have been done. Nevertheless, those who criticize shamans for being psychotic are the ones who acknowledge that the shamans' cure rates are equal to Western expectations.

When turning to the standard works in culture and personality, we find that the medicine man is typed similarly; that is to say, he is regarded as displaying neurotic if not psychotic tendencies by no less leaders in the field than Hallowell (1955), Honigmann (1959), LaBarre (1970), Roheim (1950), and Wallace (1961), to cite only a small portion of those anthropologists concerned with the relationships among cultures from a psychological perspective.

Even when anthropologists have deviated from the culture and personality norm, making claims that they could find nothing abnormal about shamanistic behavior (such as Elkin tor Australian aborigines [1964]), it is rebutted by one defender of the psychotic-shaman school who says, "It must be confessed . . . that the qualification of some anthropologists to make psychiatric assessments is open to question" (LaBarre 1970, 317).

It is as if the shaman and all his cultural counterparts are doomed to conceptual incarceration in the locked wards. Clearly the modern-day medicine man cannot win.

RITUAL CURING AT PINE RIDGE

Historically, the Lakota are well known because of their conquest of the Plains, their annihilation of Colonel George Armstrong Custer and part of the Seventh Cavalry, and their participation in the Ghost Dance religious movement of 1888–90 that culminated in the Wounded Knee Massacre in December, 1890. In 1973, Wounded Knee was again occupied by members of the American Indian Movement for seventy days that ended in the death of two persons.

The Pine Ridge people, who call themselves Oglala, are perhaps equally well known for the numerous psychological studies that have been plied on them, not the least of which is one by the distinguished neo-Freudian Erik Erickson, who along with his colleagues has done more, in the view of the Oglala, to malign or at least misunderstand Lakota people (a goodly number of cultural traits seem to have been invented for the purpose of analyses).[2] Some of the more preposterous hypotheses have unfortunately become embedded uncritically in the anthropological literature. And it is no wonder today that the Lakota express some justifiable hostility toward anthropologists and treat them as the symbol of all outside interference, even though most of the research today is being done by educators.

My focus is on ritual curing, and particularly a form called Yuwipi, which in Lakota means 'to wrap up as a ball of yarn'. The modern-day medicine man of whom I speak is the ritual leader of Yuwipi, and his job is to cure his patients of "Indian sickness," conceptually a category of illnesses perceived to have afflicted Indians before the arrival of the European and the American. What the Yuwipi man, as he is called locally, does for his patient is an alternative to what the non-Indian doctor does for Indians suffering from "Whiteman sickness," a category of illnesses believed by Indians to have been brought by the Euro-Americans.[3]

Both Indian and non-Indian doctors are capable of diagnosing and treating (the Indians would say "curing") somatic and psychosomatic disorders. Among the Oglala, somatic disorders are treated by a number of specialists who prescribe herbs, diets, physical therapy, etc., and who at one time also treated wounds and broken bones. These specialists, some of whose functions have been replaced by Western physicians, are called literally, "medicine men." The Yuwipi man who specializes in the supernatural curing of psychosomatic disorders is a type of medicine man. Among the Western-trained physicians who serve the Oglala through the U.S. Public Health Hospital are also specialists who treat Indians and, to a lesser degree, non-Indians (because of hospital rules) for mainly somatic disorders and, until recently (and less successfully) psychosomatic disorders.

The alternatives of Yuwipi are important in a commmunity that otherwise eschews modern psychotherapeutic techniques. And there are many reasons why modern psychiatry has been underutilized by the Oglala and other Indian tribes.

First, the accusation found in non-Indian communities that psychiatry and psychiatrists represent the upper and middle classes is echoed by American Indians. Indians claim that psychiatrists look down on Indians, patronize them, look at them as if they were curiosities. To a lesser extent, psychiatrists, when they are present on federal reservations, administer their services through the local Public Health Service Hospital, and Indians accuse them and other physicians of "practicing" on them.

Second, there is the claim that a language barrier exists between Indian and psychiatrist, and this must be reevaluated. My own research indicates that any person requiring psychotherapy at Pine Ridge speaks English. Monolingual Lakota speakers would go to a medicine man.

Third, being a part of the Indian Health Service, psychotherapists, like other physicians, are temporary; two or three years are about the average stay. At Pine Ridge they live in what is locally called the "compound," a neighborhood of moderate homes adjacent to the hospital but isolated from the rest of the reservation community and from Lakota culture.

Fourth, Indians, who are well aware of mental illness by any cultural definition, refer to psychiatrists as "crazy" doctors; there is a stigma attached to seeing psychiatrists for the same reason as in non-Indian society. This is underscored by the fact that social control on the reservation is partly established through gossip, and patient privacy is unheard of. Indians are afraid of being seen entering the psychiatrist's office because they will be labeled "crazy."

It should be noted also that there is an absence of privacy in the alternate psychotherapies perceived as Indian. In fact, the rituals are very public. However, there is no stigma to the latter case because they are culturally relevant and because the illness is not *named* in the same way. Indians who go to psychiatrists are crazy, but Indians who go to medicine men are simply Indians with problems believed to be due to external forces such as breaking taboos and witchcraft, but not sick brains.

Fifth, there is a general feeling that cures should be effected almost immediately. This holds for somatic as well as psychosomatic treatment. After all, the Yuwipi man always cures his patients, and in a relatively short time. There is a feeling that because the medical staff at the hospital is frequently comprised of medical students they simply do not know what they are doing. Thus medical tests are regarded as proof that the physician does not understand the patient's problem.

Sixth, the conceptual, class, or physical isolation of the psychiatrists and other medical staff is viewed by the Indians as showing a lack of concern or understanding for the patient. After nearly a century of Indian-white doctor-patient relationships, what Indians know about white physicians and what physicians know about Indian patients is negligible. There is some indication that the bureaucracy of the Indian Health Service is much to blame and that there were actually firm relationships established between "family" doctors and Indian families before the IHS was established.

Finally, there is a pragmatic consideration, one that is possibly the strongest source of frustration for the Western physician. Most physicians employed by the USPHS are beginning their careers fresh out of medical schools. They look extremely young to the Indians, and in traditional Lakota culture, youthful appearance is correlated with an absence of knowledge. In a society where knowledge is equated with old age, Public Health doctors simply cannot know what they are doing, from an Indian point of view. From a doctor's point of view, this is all very frustrating. Physicians, after going through training and residency, during which time they are acknowledged experts in their field, cannot understand why patients will not follow their instructions and will curse at them, refuse to take their word, and tell them that they are incompetent.

This is partly a fault of USPHS and a long history of negativism between physicians and Indian patients and must be regarded as a symbolic statement about federal government–Indian relations and the hopelessness of the reservation. Interestingly, such bad feelings between white doctor and Indian patient do not exist in small towns or elsewhere off the reservation.

There has been no regular psychotherapist on hand since 1968; thus Indians in need of Western psychotherapeutic help either voluntarily or by referral most frequently seek help from the physician at the hospital—at least in an emergency. This, of course, adds strain to an already understaffed hospital, one whose white personnel are constantly under racist attack by militant Indians. To a steady flow of accidents, gunshot wounds, and pregnancies are added cases of violence and hysteria, often threatening or endangering the physician's life. It is essentially the reverse of what Sapir saw as the relationship between general medicine and psychiatry: "No wonder that the more honest and sensitive psychiatrists have come to feel that the trouble lies not so much in psychiatry itself as in the role which general medicine has wished general psychiatry to play" (Sapir 1966, 144).

Although Indian and non-Indian categories of illness and health do not correspond precisely, there has been an agreement until recently that the Yuwipi man (like his non-Indian counterparts) is primarily a diagnostician. When an Indian becomes ill, he seeks out the services of a Yuwipi man who, through various personal rituals such as praying with a sacred pipe, is capable of determining whether his patient suffers from Indian or Whiteman sickness. If the diagnosis is the latter, the patient is sent to the USPHS. But if the diagnosis is Indian sickness, the Yuwipi man is "retained." In either case, the Yuwipi man is placed in a rather enviable position vis-à-vis the patient's prognosis: If it is an Indian sickness, the Yuwipi man cures him and usually over a short period of time, say, one to four one-hour rituals. If the patient is cured by a white doctor, then the Yuwipi man still takes credit for having made the proper diagnosis. If the patient dies, it is the white man's fault for not having had the skill to cure the patient of an illness that, after all, was the product of the white man's society anyway. Strictly speaking, by definition, sufferers of Indian sickness never die.

Thus the medicine man not only provides an alternative form of psychotherapy but often emerges as in direct competition with the Western practitioner. Although modern psychoanalytic practice has not made great inroads in the treatment of American Indian patients, it is time perhaps to explore the relationships between the kind of treatment offered by the medicine man and that offered by the psychotherapist trained in Western medicine to see to what extent there is hope for complementarity. Although both practitioners have about the same rate of success in their respective treatments, things are beginning to change. What emerges as an important alternative desperately in need of understanding today is that the modern medicine man is no longer satisfied to cure the illnesses of his people but is slowly moving into the domain of the Western-trained psychiatrist and, more alarmingly, the domain of Western somatic medicine where such illnesses as cancer, diabetes, tuberculosis, and heart disease, all white-man sickness, have become the subject of Indian curing. I shall return to this idea later on. I should like to take a closer look first at the nature of the modern medicine man and then at the most popular form of alternative psychotherapies.

THE MODERN-DAY MEDICINE MAN

All contemporary medicine men and, according to what we can gather from historical literature, all those of the past become medicine men through an identical processional model.[4]

It begins with:

1. Mystical experience. The experience usually comes when he is a child of perhaps nine to twelve.

2. Misfortune. Usually in middle age, a man becomes ill or injured and has communications with ghosts and hears voices. There is some recognition that this misfortune is somehow related to an original, mystical experience.

3. Consultation. An ultimate need for interpretation of the mystical experience and related misfortune leads the candidate to an established medicine man.

4. Crying for a vision. The candidate undertakes the famous vision quest, known in Lakota as *hanbleceya*. A sacred place such as a hill is chosen, and the candidate is placed on it by a medicine man. The candidate stays one to four days and nights and has a vision. The medicine man interprets the vision, in some cases telling the candidate that he should become a medicine man.

5. Apprenticeship. The candidate who wishes to become a medicine man learns sacred lore from an established ritual specialist.

6. Ordination. The candidate becomes a medicine man in his own right, usually without ceremony; he simply one day begins to practice independent of his intercessor. He continues to go on vision quests to gain and maintain power until he gets older.

7. Abdication. After another misfortune or the loss of a wife or family and perceived taunting by ghosts and other spirits, the medicine man begins to close his clientele and eventually believes himself to have lost all power. Another, younger medicine man appears on the scene.[5]

Now I should like to briefly describe the Yuwipi ritual or an ideal model. Each medicine man performs his own unique variant of the ritual, although all of the rituals are similarly structured. A person suffering from Indian sickness seeks out a medicine man, offering him a pipe filled with Indian tobacco. The medicine man listens to the patient's symptoms and diagnoses the case as being either Indian or Whiteman sickness. If it is Indian sickness, the medicine man accepts the

Modern-day medicine men, ca. 1966. The man on the right is George Plenty Wolf, a well-known Yuwipi man. Courtesy Heritage Center, Inc.

case, and the two form a contractual bond by smoking the pipe together. The pipe is the ultimate seal of faith in this society, and to discontinue the relationship after the pipe is smoked is tantamount to a serious offense to the spirits.

An arrangement is made for the place and time of the ritual, and the medicine man instructs the patient to prepare the necessary accoutrements as well as a feast. Usually a patient's family or closest kin helps with the arrangements.

The place selected is usually a one-room house cleared of all furniture and other things regarded as offensive to the spirits. The windows are draped as is the door, so that the room at nightfall will be rendered totally dark. An electric light or kerosene lamp remains to illuminate the room at critical stages of the ritual. Before the actual meeting, all of the food is cooked, certain important paraphernalia that serve to delineate the altar will have been made, and in most cases

(unless it is an emergency, for which there are attenuated rituals) a preparatory sweat bath is taken under the direction of
the medicine man. The sweat bath is timed to conclude at
dark, and the participants move from the lodge right into the
empty room.

On the average, about thirty persons participate, and most
are in some way related to the patient. They take their places
around the outer periphery, sitting on blankets and pillows
on the floor with their backs against the wall. They chat about
local events while the medicine man and his apprentice or assistant begin building an altar in the center of the floor. Altar
designs originate in the medicine man's vision, and, therefore,
no two are quite alike. They follow a general pattern, however. The altar itself is delineated by seven cans filled with dirt
into which will be stuck 18-inch saplings to each of which has
been tied a half yard of cloth. These are called flags, or *waun-
yanpi,* and each signifies through the use of a special color: (a)
the four quarters of the universe, (b) the zenith and nadir, and
(c) the center of the universe. The last is symbolic of the self
and of the medicine man's private altar containing various
items such as shells, roots, feathers, and stones—the sum
total of which stands for all the natural elements and species
of animals and birds important for the knowledge of curing.

A further delineation of the altar is made through connect-
ing the seven cans to each other with a long string to which
405 tobacco offerings have been tied. If the string does not
reach around all the cans, forming a square sacred space, the
unfilled space is connected by means of placing sprigs of sage
end to end until the gap is closed. This is the final step in con-
structing the altar. Once the altar has been closed off, the ritual is about to begin, and the center space will be regarded as
extremely sacred inasmuch as it is here that the supernaturals
will congregate in the darkness and inform the medicine man
about the appropriate cure.

In the center of the altar, the medicine man constructs another altar out of earth from a mole's burrow that is formed
into a circle. On it, with his index finger, he outlines the face
of the patient to be cured as well as other symbols that give

him power. He also places on the altar rattles and individual offerings of tobacco. When all this has been arranged, he takes the sacred pipe, fills it with seven pinches of Indian tobacco, each pinch of tobacco corresponding to the seven directions delineated by the flags. At the conclusion, he caps the pipe with a wad of sage and places the pipe to one side of the altar, where it will remain until the end of the ritual.

The singers are seated directly opposite the medicine man, who faces west, symbolic of the establishment of the first direction in Lakota myth. It is the direction at which every ritual and prayer begins. The medicine man asks an assistant to test the darkness of the room, and thus the light is momentarily extinguished to determine whether or not the room is completely dark. The medicine man now stands and recites his *hanbloglaka* (dream talk) that in effect serves as credentials for all present including the supernaturals, of when and where he first received power to cure.[6]

After this speech, the assistant and sometimes another aide wrap the medicine man in a quilt and bind him securely with thongs, first around the fingers and hands and then around his head and arms and legs. Once secured, he is lifted up and placed face downward on a bed of sage with his head toward the south. Significantly, this type of wrapping occurs at birth when a child is swaddled in a special cradle, and again at death when the corpse is wrapped similarly in a buffalo hide and placed on a burial scaffold. To anticipate here the obvious question, the ritual death and rebirth of the medicine man are symbolic and simultaneous with the ritual death of the patient's sickness and his subsequent newfound health. In fact, the ritual process, like the practitioner, is called by the Lakota term *wapiye*, which may be glossed as 'rebirth'.

Once the medicine man is wrapped, the ritual proper begins. Here the purpose of the ritual is to invite the spirits from all corners of the universe. Some are believed to be animal helpers who live somewhere between the earth and the sky, and these, along with the spirits of deceased humans, are coaxed to the darkened room, where they will commune with

William Horn Cloud, a well-known singer who sang for numerous Yuwipi men. From the author's collection.

the medicine man and instruct on how to cure the patient. The spirits are enticed through prayer and communal singing and the potentiality of a reward, a feast of dog meat that has been placed on the altar along with the other traditional foods and a pinch of tobacco, the essence of which is located in the tobacco pouches that make up the long string of offerings delineating the altar.

It is rare that the spirits do not come when called, but there are occasions (or, more properly, conditions) that will prevent them from coming. These conditions are rooted in traditional beliefs such as the possible danger presented by a menstruating woman or the presence of sacred medals, relics, books, etc., which are in fact Christian and therefore antitraditional. Believed to render the ritual inefficacious, these conditions or objects are thought to be known to the medicine man.[8]

The arrival of the spirits is announced by the sound of

crashing rattles, which are perceived to be controlled and manipulated by the spirits themselves. One may "see" the rattles
dance through the evidence of bluish "sparks" that are emitted
from the floor, walls, and ceiling whenever the rattles touch.
The rattles are said to be dancing in time to the loud drums
played by the singers in accompaniment to the singing of the
entire congregation. The rattles finally "settle down," and the
spirits begin communing with the medicine man, who is believed to be able actually to see them despite the fact that the
room is totally dark.[9] During this part of the ritual, the medicine man and the spirits talk; soon the patient is asked to re-
veal the source of his troubles openly in the form of a confes-
sion, usually a statement of guilt about turning away from the
traditional Indian religion. Other members in the room may
also make statements about their intent to pray for the patient
and others who may be away from the reservation or in the
hospital, by hanging tobacco offerings in the hills nearby. The
patient, and any other person so desiring, is then asked to
stand in the darkness, grasp one of the flags closest to him,
and face the wall. A special curing song is sung, and the patient is touched in appropriate places—his head, arm, back,
etc.—by the spirits who, through this ritual action, cure him.

At the conclusion of the curing portion of the ritual, another
special song is sung during which the spirits "go home," but
not before they rapidly race down the string of offerings,
grabbing up the essence of the tobacco, which they will relish
when they get home. Once the spirits have left, the light is
turned on and the medicine man who was tied up in his blanket is mysteriously freed, sitting in the middle of the floor
facing west, the blanket folded neatly next to him, and the
string of tobacco that described the altar rolled up into a perfect ball—the Yuwipi. The altar is in a state of disarray; in particular, the face of the patient once etched on the subaltar
is erased. (The medicine man says that it is the face of the
patient—i.e., the sick person. The erasing of the face symbolizes the cure.)

The ritual is concluded with communal drinking of water,

the feasting on traditional foods, and lighting and smoking of the pipe by all. As the pipe passes to each person, he or she smokes (children touch the pipe if they do not ordinarily smoke), and each says *mitak' oyas'in*, a formulaic prayer that simply means "all my relations," interpreted to mean that the reason that they perform the ceremony is so that all may live a long life with their relatives.

THE BASIC ELEMENTS OF CURING

To return to Torrey's *Mind Game*, we see that the Yuwipi ritual fulfills what the author regards as the four basic components of psychotherapy:

1. A shared world view that makes possible the naming process, i.e., essentially a diagnosis—and here the major categories of illness are "Indian" and "White."

2. The personal qualities of therapists that appear to promote therapy.

3. Patient expectations of getting well, which are in-increased by such things as the commitment, pilgrimage, the therapist's belief in himself, and his reputation.

4. The techniques of therapy, which perhaps have been the focus of most cross-cultural works because of their often sharp contrast with what is perceived to be standard Western psychotherapeutic procedure

Lévi-Strauss's conclusions about the effectiveness of ritual curing are similar. He says that there is no reason to doubt the efficacy of "magic," (although we might want to choose a better term), for it always implies a belief in magic (or psychoanalysis), which has three complementary aspects:

> [F]irst, the sorcerer's belief in the effectiveness of his techniques; second, the patient's or victim's belief in the sorcerer's power; and, finally, the faith and expectations of the group, which constantly act as a sort of gravitational field within which the relationship between sorcerer and bewitched is located and defined. [Lévi-Strauss 1963c, 62]

Here if we read (instead of "sorcerer") "psychotherapist" and assume that the patient (but perhaps not "victim," a term left over from earlier sociology) [10] believes in the psychotherapeutic cure—after all, the patient in our own terms must be committed to the cure before it can work—and, finally, if we substitute "society," or at least that segment of society that believes in the psychotherapeutic cure for "the group," then the principal members of the magical triumvirate are synonymous with those principal characters of the psychotherapeutic community.

Here it is implicit that the shaman or sorcerer essentially undergoes the same psychosomatic states as his patient. In fact, he must, as Lévi-Strauss states, beginning with,

> first, that of the shaman himself, who, if his calling is a true one (and even if it is not, simply by virtue of practicing it), undergoes specific states of a psychosomatic nature; second, that of the sick person who may or may not experience an improvement of his condition; and, finally, that of the public, who also participate in the cure, experiencing an enthusiasm and an intellectual and emotional satisfaction which produce collective support, which in turn inaugurates a new cycle. [Lévi-Strauss 1963c, 173]

From a functional point of view, all therapies are similar. It makes no difference whether or not the procedure for curing the patient is called psychoanalysis or ritual curing, for, in the long run,

> the value of the system will no longer be based upon real cures from which certain individuals can benefit, but on the sense of security that the group receives from the myth underlying the cure and from the popular system upon which the group's universe is reconstructed. [Lévi-Strauss 1963c, 178]

And who would argue that the psychotherapist, like Lévi-Strauss's sorcerer, "did not become a great shaman because he cured his patients; he cured his patients because he had become a great shaman" (Lévi-Strauss 1963c, 174).

CONCLUSION

Perhaps all psychotherapists have too much faith in a perceived relationship between etiology and ultimate cure. The relationship is more flexible than we once thought. Certainly, one would expect a middle-class white person suffering from the perplexities emerging from the industrial revolution to seek help from a Western-trained psychotherapist—not an Indian armed with two rattles and an army of animal helpers. And surely the Indian who is depressed and anxious over a new world that has been created for him (essentially consequent upon the same industrial revolution) will not settle for a leather couch over one end of which is slouched a bearded man with a Viennese accent—such is the nature of both stereotypes. The Indian will opt for the rattles and animal helpers.

This is obviously too simple a picture to paint for the contemporary scene, or for the future. What has arisen since the mid-1970s is another kind of modern-day medicine man, one who uses what he perceives to be the traditions of his Indian people to practice medicine with hopes of curing his Indian—*and white*—patients of not only Indian sickness but also Whiteman sickness; this would include cardiovascular disease, diabetes, and even cancer. And his therapy—another kind of faith healing—is perceived to work, for today many medicine men have tape recorded testimonies from Indian and non Indian patients who attest to the "fact" that the Indian medicine man is able to cure them when the white doctor fails.

In his alleged ability to cure a patient, Indian or non-Indian, by traditional curing rituals such as Yuwipi (all of which are essentially psychotherapeutic), the medicine man does not see himself in effect as curing sickness, and here is where Indian and non-Indian categories of illness diverge. It is not the *elimination* of a disease such as cancer for which the medicine man strives. Although the patient survives the transformation of sickness to health in the ritual, he *ultimately* dies. But for the modern medicine man, so does everyone eventually, and there is no perceived relationship between the short-term ritual and long-term curing process. Everyone who partakes of the medicine man's cure lives—several times—before he dies.

The curing of the Whiteman sickness by a modern Indian medicine man is a matephor of conquest of the white man himself, not of sickness per se. It is furthermore a statement couched in the sacred language of ritual itself that underscores the real need of Indian people to be freed of dependency on the white man's hospitals, the white man's doctors, and the white man's cure, all of which are regarded as structural features of the white man.

Thus, the medicine man's cures are always effective, because it is not the individual that is cured, but Indian society itself that is methodically and patiently constructed de novo at the beginning of each Yuwipi ritual. It is through the construction of an altar to be used consciously for the doctoring of an individual and through the efficacy of the ritual process that the "group's universe is reconstructed." Simultaneously, the white man's work and all its implications for Indian people are destroyed through an unending stream of constructions and deconstructions, thus fulfilling the collective longing for a better world. It is, after all, through the superiority of the Indian over the white man—metaphorically displayed through the medicine man's ability to combat both Indian and non-Indian illness—that the Indian universe survives.

CHAPTER 7

BEYOND THE VISION: TRENDS TOWARD ECUMENICISM IN AMERICAN INDIAN RELIGIONS

ECUMENICISM is a term normally associated with trends in contemporary religion whose ultimate goals are to transform once-parochial messages into universals.[1] In the process, spiritual ideas once perceived to be in the singular domain of a particular religious body are freely transmitted to another with hope or agreement that there will be some form of reciprocity. People whose ideas were perceived to be at one time noticeably different from their own are now made more acceptable through a conscious crusade, one might say, to underscore the benefits of being similar. The only real difference between ecumenicism and syncretism, for which the former might under some circumstances be mistaken, is the degree of consciousness or unconsciousness, choice or mandate, that transpires in the process of ecumenicizing.

Ecumenicism also is frequently associated with monotheistic movements. The spiritual leaders of these movements often announce with great conviction that an ecumenical movement is about to take place, or that parochial interests are being diminished, usually for the sake of mankind, in order to bring about that more perfect world we have all been waiting for. What I would like to discuss is the relationship between ecumenicism and contemporary American Indian religions. I believe we can begin to identify some trends that reflect more adequately the original intention of the Greek work *oikoumenos* 'the inhabited world.' Once the vision has cleared, that is, the vision that we all (both native and analyst) seek in our quest for a better understanding of American Indian religions, we can ask meaningful questions about contemporary religion that have not been asked before. I would like to discuss what I think is waiting beyond the vision and to suggest that it is time to see contemporary American Indian religion, not as a category of ritual and belief narrowly located in the minds of individual tribes, or as a form of religious statement in constant juxtapositon with various North American belief systems stemming from Judaeo-Christian thought, but as a true ecumenical system of ideas that has reached all parts of the inhabited world. This ecumenical tradition is not new, but we are not quick to grasp new trends in American Indian cultures until they have become too obvious to ignore. I think there is a natural relationship among tribal religions, intertribal religious practices, and a newly emerging international religious movement based on a number of North American tribal and intertribal ideas. I think that these categories of religious behavior influence one another, and I would like to tell you how I perceive them at the moment.

Social behavior in pluralistic societies such as the United States has always presented itself as an anomaly. It is as if there were an unwritten sociological law that when peoples from various diversified cultures come together and get to know each other through participation in the educational and work place, they begin to integrate their ideas, intermarry, rear a kind of culturally hybrid family, and ultimately homogenize, desisting as culturally distinct populations.

If there is such a law, people either are ignorant of it or consciously break it every day—every generation —and any sociological theory that attempts to account for contemporary social interaction must accede to a more powerful theory, one that explains how and why socially and culturally disparate populations continue to define and redefine the parameters of their own social boundaries. The modern paradigm of social theory today begs a new question. Rather than asking, "What is the process whereby socially diverse groups become homogenized into the larger society?" the new question is, "What is the process whereby socially diverse groups, when

faced with the prospect of homogenization, attempt consciously to create a more satisfying culture, one perceived to
be different from the dominant one?"[2]

The subject of this chapter is an extension of an idea I presented in an earlier work (Powers 1977) in which I demonstrated that, despite hundreds of years of attempts by the federal government to force American Indian peoples to conform
to a Euro-American form of government, tribes continue to
maintain a sense of social identity that they perceive to be
radically different from mainstream American society. Of
course, "mainstream" is equally difficult to define in a pluralistic society such as our own, yet it is a word that everyone
seems to understand and one that the federal government has
used widely in expressing the goals of those government
agencies charged with the administration of Indian affairs.

Proposed in the earlier book was a temporary embargo on
so-called acculturation and assimilation studies so that scholars might look for a moment at the manner in which societies
maintain their culture and language despite daily interaction
with the larger society. This proposal was not intended to ignore the fact that today American Indians by and large speak,
dress, work, dwell, transport themselves, and even pray in a
manner akin to that of non-Indians with whom they share a
region. What I did suggest, however, was that these similarities did not in themselves explain why Indians vigorously
maintain certain aspects of their traditional culture. I also
pointed out that such similarities between Indian and white
culture as dress styles, automobile preferences, and style of
living did not necessarily serve as useful indices of acculturation. I further maintained that it was important to look not
only at the manner and extent to which American Indians
adopted Euroamerican cultural traits and had become "Amer-
icanized" but also at the degree to which American Indians
had employed Euro-American culture in such a way as to "In-
dianize" them.[3]

Specifically, my interest was in religion and the manner
in which traditional Oglala religious practices impinged on
modern religion despite the influences of Christianity. In

comparing the myths and rituals of Lakota culture over the past two hundred years, one could easily see that contemporary culture was still, to a large extent, based on a cosmological and ritual charter established long before Christianity.

I also argued that it is useful in any study of culture change to observe those aspects of culture that *persist*, that is, to give equal time to studies of continuity in culture. I continue to believe that many American Indian tribes, if not all peoples, not only adopt new technologies because they are forced to by the dominant society but select certain kinds of technologies over others because they serve to enhance certain aspects of their traditional culture, those that seem most likely to become dysfunctional. Here I want to make it clear that by technology I mean any ideas foreign to a subordinate group of people that somehow may be used to meet the needs of everyday living, and not necessarily industry, machines, and laboratory inventions. In this sense, technology is interchangeable with Ellul's notion of Technique, i.e., the totality of methods rationally arrived at and having absolute efficiency in every field of human activity, one that is new and sharing no common measure with the past (Ellul 1964).[4]

I should add that every social group has rationally arrived at technologies that address themselves to everyday vicissitudes, but here I am concerned with new technologies, particularly those introduced to American Indians by white people. I also recognize that all societies exhibit some characteristics of "post-traditional societies"[5] and that "political movements which come to be labeled *nationalistic* are always revolutionary in their grand objectives, but they are fairly consistently backward-looking rather than forward-looking" (Leach 1972, 80).

It is precisely this looking backward or, more appropriately, belief in the past, that permits a society to maintain its own conceptual borders. All societies do it, even our own, preoccupied as it is with reliving our western frontier history. It seems almost ironic that our focus on rugged individualism prevails in a nation in which individuals are actually constrained by their dependence on local, state, and federal government plans and policies.

Each society, however, selects its own medium for confirming beliefs about the past. For some, it is myth and ritual; for others, music and dance. The medium may be literature, photography, or computers, which at the touch of a button spew out interpretable and thus meaningful symbols. But contrary to McLuhan's fanciful notion (which on the surface seems intuitively to be right), the medium is *not* the message, at least not in all cases. In fact, the same medium is quite capable of presenting multifaceted, polysemous messages whose meanings shift resiliently, depending on the cultural conditioning of its senders and receivers.

The medium that has interested me the most is religion. But what never occurred to me in the past—given that I saw Amerindian religions more or less struggling to persist in the United States—was the continuous, persistent influence many tribal religions were to have on diverse peoples of the inhabited world.

For nearly thirty years we have been arguing over the relative merits of such terms as tribalism, nativism, pan-Indianism, revivalism, and revitalization without properly seeing that all these concepts are linked together in a very special ways. In an earlier paper I talked about a model of cultural interaction that described music and dance on the Great Plains but also had some utility in explaining and understanding other cultural domains.[6] I noted a relationship between a model of culture called tribalism, one that we study usually from a historical perspective in the United States, and intertribalism, my preferred synonym for the often-abused concept of pan-Indianism. My argument was essentially that these two categories of culture are not separable but rather stand in a dialectical relationship with each other. Tribalism as a model is a means of understanding a singular culture, or one perceived somehow to be distinct; from the point of view of continuity, tribalism is always a system for drawing meaningful lines from the past without interruption through the present and into the future. Intertribalism as a model, however, represents change, particularly rapid change. The continuity of tribalism is always in a dialectical relationship with the change of intertribalism. The former is a means of making statements about relationships among members of the same tribe; the other was a means of making statements about relationships among Indians of different tribes as well as statements about interactions between all Indians and non-Indians. People—that is, as far as this original model is concerned, Indian people—move easily between these two models, and although their coexistence may have been complex and frustrating to the analyst, Indian people themselves are quite capable of understanding the differences between tribalism and intertribalism, and also of understanding the relationship between them.

From the perspective of religion, tribalism signifies discrete systems of myth and ritual that were and are believed to be the private domain of specific tribal cultures, or at least of restricted geographic regions. Intertribalism, however, seems to be the domain of such multitribal institutions as the Native American church. At one time, it was largely believed that these two groups of religious ideas were incompatible; peyotists did not participate in tribal religion, and the reverse was true. Furthermore, although it was recognized that Indians might participate simultaneously in a native religion and a Christian denomination, it was not generally regarded as significant to see Indians participating in more than one American Indian religion. The idea that individuals can, in fact, successfully integrate the teachings of more than one tribal religion and that one or more tribal religions can be integrated with the Native American Church, is the first step in understanding trends toward ecumenicism in Indian religions.

Simultaneous participation in two religious systems was normally relegated to an individual's participation in a native religion and a Christian denomination. Perhaps more popular was serial participation in any number of belief systems—tribal, intertribal, and Christian. It is well noted that even

among the medicine men at Pine Ridge some served not only
as Catholic lay catechists but as Episcopalian layreaders as
well.[7] Today, there are some who participate in Pentecostal
meetings, the Native American Church, and tribal religions.
Another important trend in ecumenicism is based on marriages between members of different tribes, each of whom
may espouse a different tribal religion in addition to a Christian denomination. One can see that the permutations are
infinite.

If I may for a moment recap these central ideas: Ecumenicism
begins at home. American Indians today can belong to and
participate in native tribal religions and in intertribal religions
such as the Native American Church. They can participate in
Christianity—and in more than one sect, more than one de-
monination, if they choose. They may participate in all of
these categories of religions simultaneously or serially. Impor-
tantly, they may share the religious values of their spouses
from other tribes or even from other ethnic groups, while at
the same time sharing one or more sets of values of their own.

There can be no question that, once there is multiple participation in religious systems, doctrine, belief, myth, and ritual
are likely at some point to be confused. Lines—probably imaginary ones—that once separated one set of religious beliefs
from another become washed away, and in the middle of all
this ecumenicism we try to distinguish between the old and
the new, the true and the false. We are forced to look at the
process of invention and reinvention of cultural values and
with them myths and rituals to accompany the exigencies of
these continuities and changes. And soon we find that we
must question the very nature of American Indian religions as
Indians themselves are doing, even when it is but *one* tribal
religion whose traditional values seem to be withering away
only to be replaced by what the old people fear as a travesty of
their original way of life. We must question those beliefs
founded and fostered by the young generation of religionists
who, on so many reservations, in so many Indian communities, and in so many cities, use native religion as an imple-

ment of politics and economics, and perhaps—something
that is most vehemently eschewed by old timers—for self-
aggrandizement.

Contemporary American Indian religion in recent years has
begun to spill over into non-Indian camps. It is well known
that non-Indian Americans have participated more or less in a
number of different kinds of tribal and intertribal rituals. Anthropologists, historians, priests, nuns, social workers, and
educators are frequent visitors to private as well as public rituals to which countless non-Indians have flocked to witness
"real" Indian events. Some non-Indians have become more
serious, even forsaking their own Euro-American culture in
order to participate fully in American Indian religion. More
and more non-Indians are participating in the Sun Dance, in
ritual curing ceremonies such as Yuwipis at Pine Ridge and
Rosebud, and in Native American Church meetings. Those
who do not have the opportunity to participate in Indian
events on the reservations or in Indian communities frequently have built sweat lodges on their land—even in their
back yards—and occasionally seek out lonely hills for vision
quests with or without the supervision of an itinerant medicine man who is usually easily found today in major cities of
the world. Ceremonies are being held in big cities and sub-
urbs. Those non-Indians who sought eastern philosophy in
the 1950s and 1960s are discovering that they need not stray so
far from home to experience a belief system that in some way
satisfies them more than their own.

Perhaps the real surprise of ecumenicism is found in the
current trend to adopt American Indian religious ideas in
other parts of the world, particularly in Europe. There is virtually no European country, west or east, that does not have
some kind of formalized American Indian support group, as
these are known, organized to lobby on behalf of the American Indian. These are not the Europeans who grew up exclusively under the writings of Karl May, although perhaps
everyone in Central Europe is influenced by his imagination.
These are individuals who have had personal contact both in
Europe and in the United States with members of various

tribes and who, for one reason or another, identify with American Indian cultures, both personally and collectively. Although much of this behavior is no different from that exhibited by American Indian hobbyists in our own culture— which is to say there is an emphasis on the social and secular aspects of contemporary Indian culture—much of it is inextricably linked with support of political and economic issues that are themselves difficult to divorce from religious beliefs. I am thinking in particular about certain land claims dealing with sacred shrines. The issues are at once economic, political, and religious. The American Indian support groups are in constant contact with American Indian leaders both secular and sacred. They entertain these leaders in the great capital cities of Europe and are indeed interested in and concerned about the "plight" of their Indian heroes. The support groups are active in public relations campaigns, advertise their concerns in public and private periodicals and on television, and circulate petitions aimed at persuading the United States government to honor often abrogated treaties with the sovereign tribes. Favorite meeting places have been Geneva and Paris, where Indians along with members of other indigenous groups meet representatives of the United Nations nongovernment organizations and argue their cases concerning land and water rights as well as civil rights with representatives of international committees and courts. According to a paper published by Dr. Peter Swarzbauer of the Austrian American Indian Support Group[8] the group has been active and supportive of Lakota claims related to the Black Hills.

The Austrian group has contacts with the "Four Directions Council," an alliance of tribes with United Nations Nongovernmental Organization (NGO) status, and the "Traditional Elders Circle," an association of representatives from many Indian tribes. There are also personal relationships among the Austrians and the Oglala Lakota, Hopi, Cree, Mimac, Southern Cheyenne, and Innuit—many of whom visit Europe regularly.

The type of support falls into three categories: (1) public relations, in which American Indians are encouraged to speak for themselves at gatherings organized by these support groups; (2) direct support, which takes the form of financial contributions available to Indian politicians fighting for civil rights; and (3) cultural exchange, which is the least developed but does encourage improvement of relationships between Austrians and members of American Indian tribes.

Although what I have described is based mainly on Austrian support groups, similar groups have been established in all European countries. These people are serious, they are dedicated, and they are effective in spreading to their constituencies the most current information about the ongoing developments in American Indian issues.

Within those support groups are individuals who have recently become followers, adepts, of contemporary American Indian religions. Not only do they support American Indian religious freedom, but they believe in the religious precepts that they support. They do so for many reasons. Polish experts claim that young Poles identify with the ongoing oppression of American Indians. Hungarians dress up and emulate what they have come to know as contemporary Indian ceremonies. Germans see some relationship between the nomadic peoples that settled their country and the American Indians. Italians see American Indians as the only oppressed group that actually fought and, in some cases, won battles with their oppressors. In France, England, Finland, Sweden, Norway, Denmark, and Belgium, similar Indian causes are popular.[9]

The movement, if it can be called that, is certainly small—but it is ecumenical in its intent and its practice. In Pisa, Italy, there are currently sixteen books on American Indians being translated into Italian. They are not for scholarly consumption; they are for the masses. And Black Elk, who had already reached some prominence in France, has arrived in Rome!

These brief comments perhaps do not do justice to the amount of interest being shown in Europe. I hope they do provide a backdrop for other comments I want to make about ecumenical movements outside Indian America. With every ecumenical movement, there is a hope that parochial interests will desist, that there will be new understanding, a new hope, a feeling that the world will be a little better because of some rediscovered unity of mankind. But, in all ecumenical movements there are also some disadvantages; after all, it is not that easy to promote unity on the basis of beliefs that belong to someone else. In keeping with the phenomenon of ecumenicism everywhere, the spread of American Indian religion on a worldwide basis is not without its problems. I should like to consider those problems related to the European spread of American Indian religion, problems related to ecumenicism among non-Indians in the United States, and also problems pertaining to American Indians themselves. All of these movements revolve around a worldwide interest in American Indian religion, but what precisely is the nature of the religion being disseminated? By whom is it being disseminated? And who are the benefactors?

Although regular visitors to Europe have included members of several different tribes, the most frequently emulated religious behaviors are clearly those of the Northern Plains. Of course, this is true in non-Indian America, too. It is in Lakota Sun Dances that most white people participate, and it is largely Lakota leaders who have promoted off-reservation Sun Dances such as those held in California.

There is evidence that the United Nations itself has fostered some of the ecumenicism through the creation of an alliance of Indian tribes with NGO status; the United Nations role in the so-called liberation of native peoples is not without historic precedents in Europe and America. One is quick to wonder whether or not ecumenicism is becoming simply another means for maintaining the stereotype of the noble red man, an image that supports great concern among Europeans who now see themselves as part of the contemporary struggle to defend native land and water rights. Religious freedom, of course, is reserved by Europeans for "traditionalists," a term becoming increasingly popular in the United States, but one that is imbued with many different meanings. Not only is it difficult to understand just what traditionalism means in the United States, but the term becomes even more blurred when it crosses the Atlantic. Europeans perceive traditionalists as being somehow more *real* than other Indians, in fact, more *Indian*. The European image of the traditional Indian, though it is couched in contemporary terms of current struggles for retention of land rights, water rights, sovereignty, and religious freedom, is not much more than a new version of the noble red man, although not admittedly so. Clearly, while the intent of some European scholars is to destroy the myth of the noble red man, others are in fact recreating an even stronger, nobler image. This is perhaps because European studies of American Indians tend to be interdisciplinary, and a goodly number of scholars pursue American Indian studies as a branch of American literature. Those involved in literature have a much greater influence on the kind of literature that is published than, say, anthropologists and historians.

If we look at the titles being translated into roughly nine European languages,[10] we find that European publishers are much like their American counterparts in that titles having sold well in the United States and Canada are given preference over those that have not. Since it is the popular market that publishers have in mind, we are not surprised (or are we?) to find leading the list such works as those by Carlos Castaneda, Hymeyohsts Storm, the autobiography of Red Fox, Charles Eastman, Luther Standing Bear, Leslie Silko, John G. Neihardt, Joseph Epes Brown, and N. Scott Momaday—that is, a fair mixture of the best and the worst. The struggle the European seeks to support is frequently based on uninformed ideas about American Indians, most of which are traceable to the noble image that these same supporters seek to demolish. Yet, even in the political sphere that rarely can be detached from the religious one, there is frequently a naïve grasp of contemporary problems. For example, in a form letter addressed to Chief Justice Warren Berger an anonymous writer makes the following comments:

> I am writing to you because I feel personally outraged by what the Federal Courts are doing in the United States in allowing the State of South Dakota to destroy Bear Butte as well as to deny the Lakota people access to this important religious shrine. . . . The Lakota have used Bear Butte since time immemorial. It is

the most sacred shrine, since it is the place where the people received their original instructions from the Creator similar to the way Moses received the Ten Commandments. Lakota use the Butte for the vision quest, a religious ceremony where they can come into direct contact with the spiritual world and receive guidance to last them throughout life. Complete solitude is necessary and essential to complete this ceremony. . . . Your courts have now allowed the State of South Dakota to make a zoo out of the Lakota's shrine, where tourists can come to photograph and disrupt religious ceremonies. We in Europe feel a sense of outrage. Your Government claims one thing and your courts act in contradiction to it. This is contradicting the image the United States are trying to create internationally as a nation advocating human rights.[11]

One wonders, of course, just how supportive these kinds of demands can be, particularly at a time when the issues are being contested legally elsewhere. I am thoroughly aware that American Indians have lost crucial issues in the American court system, and I am aware that sentiments run strongly against this system. But I am not convinced that European governments, or their constituents, who have in fact no vested interest in the American Indian except perhaps a sympathetic understanding from afar, can do anything except possibly make matters worse by reverting to and relying on noble images as a means of defending the rights of Native Americans.

Fortunately, different groups of Europeans approach American Indian studies in different ways. For example (in addition to those interests mentioned earlier):

• In the Soviet Union, not only are North American Indian specialists meeting under the auspices of the Institute of Ethnography of the Academy of Sciences of the USSR, but young Soviets have since 1982 formed an American Indian club that holds powwows outside Leningrad.

• A new enthusiasm for American Indian studies, including the reenactment of sacred rituals, can be found in Czechoslovakia. Indianists publish a newsletter called *Tipi* that features, among other things, lessons in the Lakota language.

• A magazine called *De Kiva* is published by the American Indian Workgroup in the Netherlands and Belgium. It is twenty years old, and twice a year on Kiva Day eighty to 100 members gather to attend lectures and slide presentations on various historic and contemporary aspects of American Indians.

• In 1973 another Netherlands action group was formed in conjunction with the American Indian Movement occupation of Wounded Knee. It is divided into twenty local groups that lecture to schools and churches and collect money for Indian causes. It also publishes a monthly journal, *Nanai.*

• The German American Indian Group (GAIG) publishes a slick magazine called *Amedian* which is devoted mainly to current political and economic issues in Indian America. It attempts to correct false images of American Indians in Germany and to "help Native Americans to realize a revived Indian America." [12]

• The most informative publication, from the perspective of all of Europe, is the newsletter (begun in 1980) of the American Indian Workshop, a division of the European Association of American Studies, edited by Christian F. Feest, of the Museum für Völkerkunde, Vienna. There is no question that Vienna is the new Indian capital of the West—western Europe, that is. The American Indian support group in Vienna has been host to American Indian visitors for several years. Some met with the chancellor of Austria in 1983 in an attempt to encourage the Austrian government to back American Indian people living in a "tribal state." A year earlier, Count Arnold Keyserling formally inaugurated the first European earth shrine designed by a self-proclaimed shaman, Ernst Graf, who himself was inspired by a visit from an Indian medicine man, Swift Deer.

These are but a few more examples of Indian ecumenical activities in Europe, yet they should suffice to give some idea of the great interest and concern non-American citizens have for American Indians. Yet, as sympathetic as Europeans and other non-Indian Americans might be to current American Indian political and economic issues, there continues to be an undercurrent of idealism that makes it difficult for non-Indians to disaffiliate from older notions of the noble savage. As much as the Europeans argue for a realistic attitude toward the American Indian, one that can help address problems of the twentieth century, their ability to implement such realism on the American Indian scene continues to be partly obfuscated by the inability to give up the historical ghost. Part of this problem, I think, is a matter not simply of white people wanting Indians to be somehow superhuman, graceful, noble people whose earlier life-styles should be emulated by all wishing to commune with nature and live in harmony with the world, but of Indians themselves, particularly those who make pilgrimages to Europe or to college campuses speaking on behalf of their people who also are eager to perpetuate the image.

Lest this be taken as hopeless and indefensible heresy on my part, let me add that I myself think that in some cases the noble red man does in fact exist. I believe over my lifetime, most of which has been spent with American Indians, I can truthfully say that I have met some noble Indian people—but they were individuals who for whatever reasons separated themselves from the rest of the tribe by either words or deeds and were recognized by their own people as deserving the appellation "noble." Let me also say that I believe nobility is something like assimilation—it applies well to individuals but not to entire tribes or nations.

If we can distinguish between the older concept of the noble savage, one attributed to the entire continent, and a newer one, which can be applied to individuals, we are further along in considering the American Indian in a better and more sharply defined perspective, one that is necessary to help American Indian nations eliminate prevailing political and economic problems. My strongest feeling is that the continuing image, whether it is perpetuated by non-Indian Americans, Europeans, or American Indians themselves, tends to militate against the best interests of Native Americans currently engaged in legal battles over critical issues relevant to their respective tribes. As a case in point, I think the Black Hills claim was seriously damaged by the Yellow Thunder Camp. The former seeks justification for claiming the entire

Frank Afraid of Horse. For many the image of the noble red man is associated with an earlier time. Although the term has been misused, there are contemporary Indians who certainly deserve the appellation. Photograph by David Zimmerly, taken at Pine Ridge in 1962. Author's collection.

Hills, while the second argues to defend an eight-hundred-acre section. While some of the tribal attorneys are arguing in the courts, followers of the Yellow Thunder philosophy are arguing in Geneva. Each faction creates and influences its own constituencies, often to the extent that the real issue is totally blurred.

A number of results are already beginning to take shape as these trends toward ecumenicism extend around the world. My immediate response to these trends, as I view them in certain parts of the United States and in those parts of Europe where I have had the chance to meet with Americanists, is that the American Indian is about to become even nobler in the twenty-first century than anyone could have believed he was in the eighteenth, nineteenth, and twentieth centuries. There are a number of reasons for this, and I would like to discuss only a few that I see as most important.

First, in the United States, the study of American Indian culture (and perhaps religion even more so) where it once was almost exclusively in the domain of anthropologists, has been taken over by various representatives of the humanities. The so-called significance of American Indian spiritualism, symbolism and meaning has become a major focus of scholars in American literature, comparative literature, poetry, linguistics, semiotics, structuralism, comparative religion, music, art, history, history of religions, psychology, and education. Certainly I am aware that anthropology has adopted all of these disciplines, but I also want to underscore that when "anthropological" approaches are imposed, the disciplines themselves are transformed, sometimes to the point where the anthropological approach is no longer representative of the discipline.

Although I would not want to claim that anthropological approaches to American Indian religion are somehow more beneficial than others, I do feel it safe to say that anthropologists, until recently, have been much more descriptive than analytical in their work, owing perhaps to the great influence of Franz Boas. With other approaches, there is sometimes a great deal of difficulty in separating the more analytical descriptions of contemporary American Indian religion from the religions themselves. I think much of what we are witnessing today, particularly in the publication of books on American Indian religion (and again particularly in those being produced by literary persons, poets, and religionists) is doctrinaire. There is often a belief that there is agreement between the people writing the books and the people about whom the books are written—and that what the naïve reader is witnessing is truth.

Perhaps one of the best examples, and one that has been part of my own research for so many years, is that of Black Elk. At one time we relied on understanding what has now come to be called the "teachings" of Black Elk from John G. Neihardt's now-famous book, *Black Elk Speaks*. With Joseph Epes Brown's *The Sacred Pipe*, Black Elk's name is now invoked and I daresay revered the world over in increasing numbers of academic departments. There are, I believe, several books being published on some aspect of Black Elk, and most recently has has been praised most uncritically by several persons in an anthology. My point is not that Black Elk does not deserve to be read as literature or poetry, but I do call attention to the fact that the act of raising one medicine man above another has been traditionally regarded as heretical among native Lakota. In fact, those Lakota of Black Elk's generation and perhaps following generations were amazed that so much fuss was made over a person who, in their eyes, was just another medicine man—a term which, incidentally, connotes for the old-timers both good and bad points.

One of the problems in the continuing study of ecumenicism in American Indian religions—one that may prove to be profitable for decades to come, is to find out just how much of what passes as contemporary American Indian religion has been, in fact, created by non-Indians. In this context, the case of Black Elk is instructive.[13]

Second, the creation of Native American studies programs over the past fifteen years required the creation and implementation of still another new genre of theory and methodology. Where there are departments of Native American studies, the

faculties represent diverse backgrounds. Tribal representation—and I am not being critical here, only reflecting the reality of any new and burgeoning program—tends to be controlled at both faculty and student levels. What is taught as
Native American studies is perforce based on an agreement
about what these studies should be. Still, no one has really
determined what it is—somewhat as in the study of religion
itself. The people involved in these studies represent a fair
mix of faculty and students subjectively involved in American
Indian culture and those who are more or less objectively involved. Either way, the trend is toward an idealized notion of
what American Indian cultures have been and what they are
expected to be. These trends are particularly noticeable in urban areas where the programs are part of a university, and
less so on reservations where there are community colleges,
or now four-year colleges where the focus of Native American
studies still tends to be on tribal rather than intertribal history
and culture. Nevertheless, even in this case, much of the curriculum being offered to students is based on often idealized
if not fanciful notions of what tribal culture is—or at least
ought to be.

This is partly because it is frequently difficult to find trained
people willing to devote themselves to American Indian education in community colleges. This should in no way detract
from the number of gifted people who do. But one must come
to appreciate that frequently the trained experts in community colleges are not so much tribal elders who are willing to
share their experience of religion and other aspects of culture
with students as persons who qualify for teaching a course
simply because they have taken it. This, of course, is part of a
larger problem inherent to enclaves such as those on the large
reservations that are expected to produce quality programs
with little realistic help from the government. I am beginning
to wonder whether some kinds of education are detrimental
to Indian cultures. For example, bilingual education on some
reservations, where a good part of the students already speak
the native language, are more successful than programs on
those reservations where most of the students do not speak

the native language. In the first case, one wonders to what extent the native language is being used simply to teach English; in others it becomes evident that no amount of bilingual education, as it is currently constituted, will ever enable the students to learn their native language.[14]

Finally, I think that the greatest influence on ecumenical trends throughout the world (I include here reservations and Native American communities as well as more exotic places) is that of national and international media—and I include newspapers, radio, television, and books that will continue to shape world opinions and create images of American Indians, just as they do for all people of the world. What we are expected or even entitled to know about other peoples and other places is fairly well dictated by big business, and of course this is an irreconcilable problem. In 1983, when *The Mystic Warrior* aired on television, we saw to what extent big business co-opted American Indian culture and especially religion. This film was based on a best-selling novel, *Hanta Yo*, written by Ruth Beebe Hill and her companion Canksa Yuha (who alone, according to the publicity, was entrusted with *real* knowledge of the Lakota and Dakota people). The publisher is Doubleday, the paperback company is Warner Communications, the network is ABC, and the producer is David Wolper, the same person who brought us "Roots." Despite the fact that Lakota and Dakota who formed a loose alliance with their most dreaded enemies—anthropologists in 1978— at the time deplored the fact that the white man (and white woman) would dare produce a film out of what was considered a travesty of a book dealing with all the misconceptions of Lakota culture as well as a few that the author created herself with the aid of Canksa Yuha. In fact, all appeals, and those would include lawsuits, by Indian people were ignored. Many of us worked for years to try to stop the production of *The Mystic Warrior,* perhaps naïvely, wondering just how some kind of lesson could be learned—and for what reasons in the future—out of the power of publishers and networks to simply do what they please. Most unsettling to me, however, was the fact that, after Indian women appealed personally to David Wolper to stop production, it was American Indians themselves who supported the project and profited from it, and they still continue to do so.[15]

As I understand it, *The Mystic Warrior* will be distributed around the world—in how many languages? And there is some plan to put it into classrooms, although some of the sexier scenes will probably have to be cut. One can see that this concentrated effort by Indians and whites to turn one American Indian religion into a worldwide circus will have resounding effects on the image of the American Indian. I am not so much offended by the nature of some of the scenes; I am not being prudish about the sex scenes, nor am I being defensive about the scenes of the Sun Dance, which the Black Hills Treaty Council begged to have deleted. What worries me is that the author of the book, and those Indians and whites who joined in the support and production of the book, paperback, and film, might one day be called into a congressional hearing as expert witnesses on the Lakota. They undoubtedly have amassed a great number of credentials and respectability in the eyes of the peoples of the world who, in fact, would like to maintain the stereotype image of the American Indian to satisfy their own personal and political needs, perhaps more than they want to protect the interests of Indians themselves. Remember, once out of Indian country, the peoples of the world (and I suspect that would include Native Americans who travel the world in search of support) no sharp distinctions are drawn between Black Elk and Red Fox; Eastman, Standing Bear, Welch, and Momaday—they are all Indians.

I for one am concerned about the nature of this ecumenicism because I think that there is some danger in allowing it to be disseminated around the world without some critical evaluation. I think that this ecumenical movement can be used positively to assist Native Americans in struggles against unfair legislation and the aftermath of treaty abrogations. But if we are to acknowledge the vision of American Indian peoples today—whatever they are in their most diverse forms and meanings, we should be aware that the noble red man is alive and well in disparate parts of the world, and that would include our own small part of the planet—the United States.

I am not providing a program—I think American Indians are quite capable of providing their own—but I am saying that American Indian religion is being shaped before our very eyes, sometimes with the help of American Indians and sometimes not, and the result will have a great deal of bearing on contemporary issues, some of which are better decided here at home where we are all closer to the nature of the problem. I do not think that we who are truly interested in American Indian peoples can afford to allow programs—foreign or domestic—to so distort the nature of American Indian culture that they can be used against Indian tribes in their legal disputes with the United States government. I am not being naïve here—not intentionally—but I do believe that many of us, even those of us who are not Indians, can work together with American Indians or work together with white people and other non-Indians interested in American Indian causes, for those who *are* American Indians, to try to dispel some of the greatest myths now in circulation—myths that for many of us should have died out several decades ago.

Perhaps I have not raised the key issue: Why American Indians? There are countries where many ethnic groups could perhaps serve the purpose of providing ideological bases for the dominant society much better. I think that American Indians should be proud that they have been chosen by people in these countries and around the world as the symbol of political, economic, and religious persecution, a symbol to be emulated. Yet I would hope that if we were to reach beyond the vision we will see that these trends toward ecumenicism, these trends that seek to inhabit the world, should do so in such a way as to enhance the true objectives of the Native American rather than those who would emulate him.

NOTES

Preface

1. Powers 1977, 1982, 1986.

2. The special brand actually comprises several, including kinship, mythology, and "primitive" classification, or what Leach calls Lévi-Strauss's "three limbs of the star" (Leach 1970:4). For those interested in beginning an odyssey into Lévi-Strauss's logic, kinship is best treated in his seminal "Social Structure" (1962) and the monumental *Elementary Structures of Kinship* (1969a; original 1949). Mythology is scattered through much if not all of Lévi-Strauss's work. Of major importance in method is "The Structural Study of Myth" (in Lévi-Strauss 1963a). His major opus is the four-volume *Les Mythologique* (1969b, original 1964; 1973, original 1966; 1978, original 1968; and 1981, original 1971). On his ideas about classification it is best to read first Durkheim and Mauss's *Primitive Classification* (1963; original 1903), which is his own starting point, followed by *Totemism* (1963b; original 1962) and then *The Savage Mind* (1966; original 1962). Various essays, chosen by himself for republication appear in *Structural Anthropology* (1963a) and *Structural Anthropology II* (1976). One can begin studying the pros and cons of Lévi-Strauss with Leach's *Claude Lévi-Strauss* (1970), Rossi's *The Unconscious in Culture: The Structuralism of Claude Lévi-Strauss in Perspective* (1974); and Shalvey's *Claude Lévi-Strauss Social Psychotherapy and the Collective Unconscious* (1979). Of course, this would be just a beginning.

3. Buechel's best known works are *Bible History in the Language of the Teton Sioux Indians* (1924); *A Grammar of Lakota* (1939); and *Lakota–English Dictionary* (1970). The last was published posthumously and contains a brief biographical sketch.

4. For example, the opposition found in the Four Winds, and the Sky and Earth, as well as other directional symbolism, are for the Lakota empirical, not analytical. On this point see Powers (1977).

5. A discussion of early theories about the origin of music may be found in Nettl (1956).

6. This criticism is not exclusive to ethnomusicology. All fields beginning with the prefix *ethno-* suffer from similar intellectual schizophrenia. Perhaps this is an indication that it is time to drop the prefix and try harder to more solidly integrate the disciplines.

7. It should be noted that Hymes acknowledges the earlier work of Roman Jakobson, who also had a great influence on Lévi-Strauss.

8. Although anthropologists claim "participant-observation" as one of their most distinguishing features, most description and analysis is based on observations. Here I am suggesting that anthropologists might find it profitable to emphasize their own participation—where it is applicable—as part of the analysis.

9. These terminological distinctions are attributable to d'Aquili et al. (1979).

10. Obviously, it is unlikely that disciplines that study differences between people will relinquish their positions given the long-term investment they have made in establishing, proving, and maintaining their uniqueness, although many individual scholars would be happy to tear down some of the artificial boundaries separating these disciplines.

11. I am particularly indebted to a number of persons with whom I have discussed PHS operations, including Darlene Shortbull, R.N., Pine Ridge Public Health Hospital; Ronald Forgey, D.O.; Donald Forgey, J.D.; and Marla N. Powers. Naturally I am wholly responsible for my assumptions and suggestions.

12. Many of the support groups do not distinguish between traditionalist and activist, believing as many young American Indians do that the older generation categorically supports the political activism of the younger.

Introduction

1. Lakota is the acceptable designation for the people otherwise known as "Sioux." One "rational" way of solving this apparent contradiction is to assume that what is important to the old Lakota is that the sacred number 7 was resolved by adding five rituals to the two earlier ones. Significant here is not how mythology arrives at the sacred number 7 but that it arrives at 7. On the issue of numbers as predetermined structuring principles, see "Counting Your Blessings."

2. For those sensitive to the continuous use of the pronoun *he*, let me state that the vision quest was not in the purview of females until the mid 1970s. For more on the participation of Lakota women in rituals see M. N. Powers (1980, 1986.)

Chapter 1

1. This chapter was first presented in an earlier version as a paper entitled "The Structure and Function of the Vocable" at the annual meeting of the Society for Ethnomusicology, Montreal, 1979. Subsequently a revision of the paper was presented to faculty and students of the Faculté de Musique, Université de Montréal, in 1980. I would like to thank Nicole Beaudry, Charles Boiles, Jean–Jacques Nattiez, and Ramón Pelinsky for many hours of discussion of the subject, and for their warm and generous hospitality.

2. On the subject of biogenetic structuralism, see d'Aquili et al. (1979); and D'Aquili (1983).

3. Halpern has underscored the potentiality for research on the vocable (Halpern 1976). I do not deny that the vocable has been treated historically by nearly all researchers investigating Native American music. But so far there has been no attempt to offer any general theory related to its structure, function, or origin. A detailed bibliography of works on the vocable appears in Frisbie 1980. She has written the best detailed treatise to date on the significance of the vocable in Navajo music.

4. Langer is, of course, an antievolutionist. But she does contribute substantially to meaning in music, particularly in chap. 8.

5. Ethnomusicological approaches to music, even when they are predominantly anthropological, are influenced essentially by British and American functionalism, Boasian diffusionism, historical particularism, and a residual of mid-nineteenth cultural evolution, the latter of which contributes significantly to our need to distinguish implicitly or explicitly between primitive and civilized. By giving some privileged status to "natural man," we tend to agree strongly with philosophers and poets who continue to maintain a romantic relationship with the scientifically-dubious pristine stage.

6. Wilson (1975) generally would answer to paternity-certainty charges himself as "father of sociobiology."

7. Since this chapter was first presented as a lecture, there has been a rash of publications on the analysis of sound as a symbolic system. See in particular Feld 1974.

8. Here I refer to the works of Nattiez (1975) on the semiotics of music, and Feld's criticism of the faddish application of structural linguistics and structural anthropological method (1974). The vocable as subject of research seems to mediate just as nicely between ethnomusicological argument as it probably mediates between language and music.

9. List's work with the Hopi (1968) anticipates this, but perhaps for different reasons.

10. The arbitrariness with which these terms are used is indica-

tive of an absence of scientific interest in the vocable and is suggestive of its status in ethnomusicological research.

11. Some of my earliest works on the structure of vocables can be found in Powers 1961a and 1961b.

12. These are the only vowels that are nasalized in Lakota and Dakota, and for purposes of this chapter underscore the relationship between vocable and language.

13. This is owing to euphony. when the last phoneme immediately preceding the cadential formula is /a/, /e/, or /i/, *ye lo* (*yelo*) is used; when it ends in /o/ or /u/, *we lo* (*welo*). All these phonemes may be nasalized, but nasalization does not affect the choice of initial vocable.

14. *L* and *D* represent the major dialectal differences in Lakota and Dakota, but there are others.

15. Again, these phonemes are typically Ðegiha, and partly serve to distinguish this linguistic subfamily from Lakota and Dakota, as well as other subfamilies such as Chiwere and Winnebago.

16. See also Hymes's discussion of the "structural function" of the cadence in Northwest Coast songs (1965). In my analysis structures have more than one function.

17. As Baskin states, "DeSaussure was among the first to see that language is a self-contained system whose interdependent parts function and acquire value through their relationship to the whole" (deSaussure, trans. Baskin, 1959; xii; original 1906–11). This insight gives De Saussure prominence as one of the founders of modern structuralist thought.

18. I am suggesting here that "song style" may be explained in terms of switching from a signal to a symbolic mode of expression, that is, the relationship between the musical idea and its expression is arbitrary within a culturally relevant context.

19. Fletcher hinted that vocables often rhymed with each other because they appeared at the ends of phrases (1900:126). My point is that suffixed vocables rhyme with the preceding final syllables of meaningful text.

20. One of the best synthetic arguments is found in Fox 1980.

21. For a review of the status of brain research, particularly as it affects anthropoloy, see Fabrega (1977); for a review of sociobiological theories, see Williams (1981).

22. The relationship between brain and behavior, originally in the purview of neurobiologists and psychologists, has finally made some headway into social and cultural anthropology with the publication of Turner (1985).

23. This idea is based on an important theme that runs through much of the work of Robin Fox. See in particular Fox (1971).

Chapter 2

1. This chapter was presented at the First Conference on Culture and Communications at Temple University in March, 1975.

2. I refer in particular to the seminal work of Hymes (1962, 1974), to which I refer again later.

3. Most songs were at one time sung in cycles of four—a custom still prevalent on the Southern Plains.

4. At one time, ending on the last beat of the drum was not important on the Northern Plains. In fact, many Lakota songs ended without drum accompaniment, the rhythm being carried exclusively by the voices of the singers.

5. Locally, the noon meal is called dinner, and the evening meal supper.

6. Some of these song groups have been active since the beginning of the reservation period; others are quite transient.

7. "Day money" is a rodeo term adapted to the powwow. A number of other powwow features can be traced to the rodeo (Powers 1968).

8. Up through the 1950s the singers took their place in the dance area near the center flagpole, and, in effect, everyone danced around the singers. One group of singers normally sufficed for the dance. Since the 1960s, however, several groups of singers perform. They use public address systems and can easily be heard from any part of the dance area.

9. This song structure was originally presented by me in 1959 and has been since refined.

10. Most powwows today employ head dancers. Others do not begin until the head dancer is on the floor. Female head dancers are also prominent today, particularly at urban powwows.

11. "Uluating" is a term used by ethnomusicologists to describe the short, staccato tremolos emitted by rapid movement of the tongue against the hard palate resembling a shrill *li-li-li-li.*

12. Future work will include the effect of the audience on the behavior of singers and dancers.

13. These other aspects, in addition to the behavior of the audience, also should include that of the announcer who figures prominently in all powwows, as well as other principals, such as persons giving way and those given way to.

14. "Ornamentative" is an ethnomusicological term used to describe vocal sounds that are neither part of speech nor of song, such as shouts, screams, and imitations of animal sounds. It could be argued from an Indian point of view that these ornamentations are in fact integral to the song proper.

15. A classification of musical instruments that includes drums, hence, sounds or cues emanating from the drum.

16. A classification of musical instruments that includes flageolets, flutes, and whistles, hence, sounds or cues emanating from the dancers' whistles.

17. A classification of musical instruments that includes rattles and bells, hence, sounds or cues emanting from the dancers' bells.

Chapter 3

1. This paper was originally presented as part of the symposium "Neurobiology . . . does it really matter?" at a conference of the Institute on Religion in an Age of Science, August, 1984 at Star Island, New Hampshire. A revised edition was subsequently published in *Zygon* (1985). I would like to thank Eugene d'Aquili, Robin Fox, Solomon H. Katz, and Colwyn Trevarthen for useful comments on various sections of the paper.

2. d'Aquili (1983:247). See also Fox (1980), particularly chap. 7.

3. A structural analysis of Oglala myth and ritual appears in Powers (1977, 1982).

4. Claude Lévi-Strauss (1966). However, it should be recognized that the basic numbers, i.e., the constituent parts of a binary opposition, lie at the very foundation of structural analysis, particularly, Lévi-Straussian.

5. The semiotic-evolutionary distinction is made by d'Aquili, et al (1979:304).

6. d'Aquili et al. (1979:5–6) select the term "equilibration" over "equilibrium" because the former imparts the notion of "process, as opposed to equilibrium which is a state of balance."

7. I have presented this idea elsewhere with specific reference to the evolution of music in chap. 1.

8. A more recent edition is available: Lucien Lévy-Bruhl (1966) with an Introduction by Ruth L. Bunzel.

9. Lévy-Bruhl, 1966:63. Several more examples are included in chap. 5.

10. Ibid., p. 167.

11. Ibid.

12. It should be emphasized that no cross-cultural studies have yet been made.

13. There are reports that in Plains Indian sign language counting begins on the right hand. However, a distinction should be made between enumeration, an often unconscious motor response employed to aid verbal discourse; and counting proper, a conscious response applied to particular quantities. The preeminence of the right hand is correct when one is speaking of counting (in sign language), but

my example is typical of what might be called mnemonic signing, that is, enumerating things on one's fingers so as not to lose count. Interestingly, even in sign language, earlier researchers note that the sign for "hundred" is formed by extending the left hand and stroking each finger of the left hand with the right index finger, each finger of the left counting as 100. After 500 is reached, the hands are reversed; nevertheless, the process begins with an active right hand. The authority here is Tomkins (1969).

14. Solomon H. Katz, Department of Anthropology, University of Pennsylvania, has conducted a number of these studies that are not yet published.

15. Illustrations of these signs can be found in Tomkins (1969). Also see Clark (1881) and Mallery (1880).

16. I would like to thank Colwyn Trevarthen, Department of Psychology, University of Edinburgh, for sharing with me his insights on the relationship between handedness and the production of sound in instrumental music. As far as I know, no study has been made of this fascinating subject.

17. Lévy-Bruhl 1966:181.

18. Lévy-Bruhl owes much of his insights to the work of A. Bergaigne, who wrote *La réligion védique,* published in Paris between 1878 and 1883.

19. Lévy-Bruhl 1966:pp. 159–60; italics in original.

20. Bergaigne, quoted in Lévy-Bruhl. 1966:196.

21. Lévy-Bruhl 1966:196.

22. An excellent discussion of the relationship between form and content from a structuralist position can be found in Lane 1970.

23. I have raised this issue briefly in Powers (1981a:443).

24. On this position, see Powers (1977) and Walker (1917).

25. Dundes (1968). We might also consider that there are four infielders, and three outfielders, while the pitcher-catcher dyad forms a third part of the playing field. This arrangement is not unlike the tripartite division of Gothic cathedrals, and not different in principal from the Lakota system.

26. d'Aquili et al. (1979:12).

27. On this point see Robin Fox, particularly chap. 9.

28. deSaussure (1959).

Chapter 4

1. This chapter was presented at the Plains Indian Art Seminar, under the auspices of the Department of Indian Studies, Black Hills State College, Spearfish, S.Dak., July, 1981. I would like to thank the adminstration, faculty, and students for their hospitality and particularly R.D. Theisz for useful comments and discussion.

2. A reproduction of *Sioux Rider* can be found in Milton (1972).

3. "Unknown Sioux Artist" is itself a means of classification, for, as Lévi-Strauss has written, "Classifying, as opposed to not classifying, has a value of its own, whatever form the classification may take" (1966:2). I hastily add that the act of *not* classifying ("unknown") is a classification itself that clearly places the art under discussion in an inferior category.

4. A reproduction of *Woman Dancer* adorns the cover of Milton (1972).

5. One could add to this list of hypocrisies the effects of auctioning American Indian art at such prestigious institutions as Southeby's and Christie's. The cost today of "primitive" art is clearly reaching the unaffordable prices once paid exclusively for Art.

6. The arguments over the use of the term "aesthetic" with respect to "primitive" art, as well as a useful discussion of theory and method applied to the cross-cultural study of art, can be found in Jopling (1971) and Otten (1971).

7. Lévy-Bruhl (1966).

8. This is a recurrent theme in Lévi-Strauss's work; see particularly Lévi-Strauss 1969a. I think it is safe to say that American Indians would not make such a distinction between nature and culture. Nevertheless, analytically, the distinction continues to serve as a stimulating frame of reference (rather than "theory") comparable to Van Gennep's "rites of passage" (1960); Mauss's "prestations" (1967); and Hubert and Mauss's model of "sacrifice" (1964).

9. Rudolf Otto (1958).

10. Perhaps "disagree" is too strong. In fact, in the text Lévi-Strauss (1969b:19) sounds categorical in stating that "there are no musical sounds in nature, except in a purely accidental way; there are only noises." However, in a footnote immediately following this quotation, after questioning a "genetic" relation between birdsongs and music, he further states: "The so-called songs of birds are on the frontiers of language; their purpose is to express and communicate. Therefore it is still true that musical sounds are part of culture. However, the dividing line between culture and nature is not identical as used to be thought, with any of the lines of demarcation *between human and animal nature*" (p. 19n.; italics added). I am not certain why art is not found in nature in an "accidental way." However, my major point is that from a Darwinian perspective, for example, there indeed is a genetic relationship between animal sound and human sound. Darwinian theory in fact complements Lévi-Strauss's idea about mind. Lévi-Strauss takes over, in a manner of speaking, where Darwin ends, and both meet head on, in the middle of the brain. For an interesting idea about the role of Lévi-Strauss not only as structuralist but as sociobiologist, see Shalvey (1979:138–40). Elsewhere

Lévi-Strauss does see an interesting metaphorical relationship between birds and human beings (Lévi-Strauss 1966:204–205).

11. For a distinction between sacred time and profane time see Bergson's contrast between *temps* and *durée* (Bergson 1949) and Schutz's interpretation of Bergson's ideas (Schutz 1951), as well as Leach (1961).

12. Sir James Frazer (1959).

13. On the theme of virgin birth see the classic work by Leach (1969:85–122).

14. Lévi-Strauss states that "all miniatures seem to have an intrinsic aesthetic quality–and from what should they draw this constant virtue if not from the dimensions themselves" Lévi-Strauss (1966:23).

15. Published by the *Instituto per la collaborazione culturale*, Venice.

16. It should be strongly stated on this final note that not all art historians, philosophers, and curators are oblivious to these problems. My friend and colleague Christian F. Feest, of the Museum für Völkerkunde, in Vienna, informs me that the Denver Art Museum exhibited American Indian art with a captial *A* as early as 1925. For an interesting discussion of the history of the relations between American Indian art and museums, see Feest (1980). I am also grateful to Nancy Lurie for calling my attention to Herskovits's relativistic approach to Art and art predating this chapter by nearly forty years (Herskovits [1949]).

Chapter 5

1. This chapter was originally presented as "Dual Religious Organization at Pine Ridge" in the symposium "The Persistence of Native American Values on the Northern Plains," at the 75th Annual Meeting of the American Anthropological Association, Washington, D.C.

2. Dual participation is the most common. However, there are some indications that people belong to multiple religious persuasions simultaneously, e.g., Christianity, tradition tribal religion, and Native American Church.

3. See also Steinmetz (1980), who in his later work carries the idea of the pipe as precursor of Jesus Christ to extremes.

4. Just as interesting is that Black Elk's mediators Brown (1953) and Neihardt (1932) do not even mention the medicine man's activity in the Catholic church. This played a major part in the man's life even at the time these authors were conducting their interviews.

5. On the concept of translating "belief" into various languages, see Needham (1972).

6. See Goll (1940).

7. Interview with Zona Fills the Pipe and Sadie Janis, Pine Ridge, 1982.

8. The most recent figures are based on interviews with tribal representatives in 1982.

9. MacGregor is not totally accurate. An Episcopalian daughter might remain Episcopalian even if she and her Roman Catholic husband were married in a Catholic church. But he is correct when he suggests that a family may be split along denominational lines as any careful inspection of local cemeteries will attest.

10. Of course, many Oglala are married by church officials in religious ceremonies, but this does not change the exogamous principle.

11. See also Lenz (1979) for a history of the Catholic congresses among the Lakota.

12. In reality, Red Cloud was baptized by a secular priest, the Rev. J. A. Bushman, on March 9, 1884, at Pine Ridge along with 142 others. This event generally marks the beginning of Catholicism at Pine Ridge (Coffey, 1942).

13. In Lakota, *sapaun*, literally means 'to wear, or use, black'; and *skaun* 'to wear, or use, white.'

14. Even today, Lakota living at Kyle, the stronghold of Episcopalianism at Pine Ridge, are regarded as more traditional than those living in other parts of the reservation.

15. The popular belief of those contemporary Lakota who remain loyal to Crazy Horse (not all do) is that before his assasination Crazy Horse made a speech in which he pledged to the government that he would fight against their mutual enemy, the Nez Percé, until "not one Nez Percé remains." It was translated "until not one white man remains."

16. Before Oglala could receive ration books, they had to answer to the agent through an interpreter the question "Tuktel yacekiya he?" Where do you pray? The appropriate answer was "Sapaun" or "Skaun" or whatever Christian denomination), and only then would they be given rations. For the symbolic use of food at Pine Ridge, see Powers and Powers (1984).

17. With respect to retention of older religious forms, see Powers, (1977, 1982).

Chapter 6

1. This chapter was presented to the faculty and students of the Department of Psychiatry, College of Dentistry and Medicine of New Jersey, Rutgers Medical School, on April 20, 1981.

2. Erikson spent only two weeks on the reservation and based most of his information on the previous study by Gordon Macgregor (1946), a work that is equally insulting to the Lakota people because

of conclusions based on an insensitivity to any principles of cultural relativism. Erikson, for example, found mixed bloods to be more "stabile" than full bloods, a "fact" unsupportable by empirical evidence. He also states that mixed bloods referred to full bloods as "niggers" and that Oglala women constantly were preoccupied with oral stimulation, giving as an example the flattening of porcupine quills for use in embroidery by means of the teeth because of early weaning practices. All this is nonsensical to anyone who has spent time among Lakota people; nevertheless, Erikson's work on Lakota childhood (1940) remains a classic in the field.

3. These categories were introduced in Powers (1977).

4. This process, first described in Powers (1977), still obtains in 1985 according to younger medicine men with whom I have talked.

5. In many ways this parallels some of the African political systems in which the headman is replaced before he becomes too old to rule, not unlike other systems including our own in which the possibility of an interregnum is met with anxiety.

6. An analysis of dream talk and other forms of special language spoken by medicine men appears in Powers (1986).

7. According to the belief system, it is this essence of the tobacco that is smoked by the supernaturals when they return home to the hills where they live. The physical form of the tobacco remains wrapped up.

8. Years ago, when I first went to Pine Ridge, there were countless stories about supernatural creatures who would pick up a person and throw him out the window of a house. This would occur during the ritual if the person did not leave the meeting when the Yuwipi man commanded. The creature was described as wet and clammy with long hair.

9. The medicine man frequently asks his followers whether they wish to see the spirits and promises to apply medicine to their eyes to make it possible. However, I know of no instance in which the medicine man's challenge was accepted.

Chapter 7

1. This paper was first presented at the Second Conference on Native American Studies, held at Oklahoma State University, Stillwater, Oklahoma in May, 1984.

2. The "conscious creation of a more satisfying culture" is attributable to the now-classic work of Anthony F. C. Wallace, particularly his article "Revitalization Movements" (1956).

3. On this, see my *Oglala Religion* (1977). This theme has been expanded in a more recent article (Powers and Powers, 1984).

4. Original, 1954.

5. The term was coined by Eisenstadt (1972).

6. Powers (1980).

7. The medicine man and lay catechist Black Elk, made famous by Neihardt (1932) and Brown (1953), is a major example.

8. Much of the information of American Indian support groups was obtained during a trip to Europe (April, 1984). In particular, Peter Schwartzbauer, of the University of Vienna, is personally active in support work and provided much help. Also Christian F. Feest, Museum für Völkerkunde, Vienna, provided useful information, some of which appears in the *American Indian Workshop Newsletter,* which he edits.

9. References to some of these groups appear in a report of the papers presented at the American Indian Workshop, a section of the European Association on American Studies, which met at the University of Rome, April 16–19, 1984 (Breinig, 1984). In a personal communication, Nancy O. Lurie tells me that there is a special relationship with the Saami (Lapps) and the Blackfeet.

10. This information is based on personal communications with translators who attended the Rome meetings.

11. It is unknown just how many of these form leters were actually sent, but the sentiments of the anonymous letter are clear.

12. *American Indian Workshop Newsletter,* 1982 (11):21. An older journal of mainly cultural affairs is *Dakota Scout.*

13. Cf. Swann (1983).

14. This is not intended as a general criticism about all bilingual programs. On the Navajo reservation, for example, they appear to be successful; but 20 percent of the Navajos are monolingual in their native language, a rather high percentage for any tribe. There are more cases in which trained teachers and uniform, graded courses are absent. Native speakers are, of course, indispensable, but so are technically trained teachers. The former are abundant, but the latter are not, and rarely are they one at the same time.. When I asked a native speaker who taught bilingual Lakota-English what he did when he had difficulties explaining the more complex aspects of Lakota grammer, he said, "I end the lesson there."

15. A number of published accounts of the controversy exist. For a general analysis of the film's inadequacies, see Powers (1979); and for a response to Wolper's justification for producing the film, see Powers (1981b).

BIBLIOGRAPHY

Bergson, Henri
1949   *An Introduction to Metaphysics.* Indianapolis: Bobbs–Merrill Co. Original 1903.
Bowra, C.M.
1962   *Primitive Song.* New York: Mentor Books.
Breinig, Helmbrecht
1984   "Buffaloes and Bills, or Cannibals and Christians: The Club in Rome." *American Indian Workshop Newsletter* 17:1–5. Vienna: Museum für Völkerkunde.
Brown, Joseph Epes
1953   *The Sacred Pipe.* Norman: University of Oklahoma Press.
Buechel, Eugene, S.J.
1924   *Bible History in the Teton Sioux Language.* New York: Benziger Brothers.
1939   *Grammar of Lakota.* Saint Louis: John S. Swift and Co.
1970   *Lakota–English Dictionary.* Pine Ridge, S. Dak.: Red Cloud Indian School.
Buettner–Janusch, John
1966   *Origins of Man.* New York: John Wiley Sons.
Clark, William P.
1881   *The Indian Sign Language.* Philadelphia: L.R. Hammersly and Co.
Coffey, Francis J., S.J.
1942   "Historical Notes." Manuscript on deposit at the Heritage Center, Inc., Holy Rosary Mission, Pine Ridge, S. Dak.
Cooper, Margaret
1965   *The Inventions of Leonardo Da Vinci* New York: Macmillan.
Count, Earl W.
1964   Comment on Hockett and Ascher, "The Human Revolution." *Current Anthropology* 5:135–68.
Critchley, MacDonald, and R. A. Henson, eds.

1977   *Music and the Brain: Studies in the Neurology of Music.* London: William Heinemann.

Daly, Martin, and Margo Wilson
1978   *Sex, Evolution, and Behavior.* North Scituate, Mass.: Duxbury Press.

d'Aquili, Eugene G.
1983   "The Myth-Ritual Complex: A Biogenetic Structural Analysis" *Zygon* 18(3): 247–69.

———, Charles D. Laughlin, Jr., and John McManus
1979   *The Spectrum of Ritual: A Biogenetic Structural Analysis.* New York: Columbia University Press.

Darwin, Charles
1859   *The Origin of Species.* New York: Modern Library, n.d.
1871   *The Descent of Man.* New York: Modern Library, n.d.
1965   *The Expression of the Emotions in Man and Animals.* Chicago: University of Chicago Press. Original 1872.

Deloria, Vine, Jr.
1969   *Custer Died for Your Sins.* New York: Macmillan.
1973   *God Is Red.* New York: Grosset & Dunlap.

deSaussure, Ferdinand
1959   *Course in General Linguistics.* Translated by Wade Baskin. New York: McGraw–Hill Book Co. Original 1906–11.

Dundes, Alan
1968   "The Number Three in American Culture." In Alan Dundes, ed. *Every Man His Way.* Englewood Cliffs, N.J.: Prentice–Hall.

Durkheim, Émile, and Marcel Mauss
1963   *Primitive Classification.* Chicago: University of Chicago Press. Original 1903.

Eisenstadt, S. N., ed.
1972   *Post-Traditional Societies.* New York: W. W. Norton.

Elkin, A. P.
1964   *The Australian Aborigines.* New York: Anchor Books. Original 1938.

Ellul, Jacques
1964   *The Technological Society.* New York: Vintage Books.

Erickson, Erik H.
1950   *Childhood and Society.* New York: W. W. Norton.

Fabrega, Horacio, Jr.
1977   "Culture, Behavior and the Nervous System." *Annual Review of Anthropology* 6: 419–55.

Feest, Christian F.
1980   *Native Arts of North America.* London: Thames and Hudson.

Feld, Steven
1974   "Linguistics and Ethnomusicology." *Ethnomusicology* 28(2):
        197–217.
Feraca, Stephen E.
1963   *Wakinyan: Contemporary Teton Dakota Religion.* Browning,
        Mont.: Museum of the Plains Indian.
1966   "The Political Status of the Early Bands and Modern Com-
        munities of the Oglala Dakota." W. H. Over. *Museum
        News* 27(1–2). Vermillion, S. Dak.
Fletcher, Alice C.
1900   *Indian Story and Song from North America.* Boston: Small
        Maynard and Co.
Fox, Robin
1967   *Kinship and Marriage.* Baltimore, Md.: Penguin Books.
1971   "The Cultural Animal." In J. F. Eisenberg and Wilton S.
        Dillon, eds. *Man and Beast: Comparative Social Behavior.*
        Washington, D.C.: Smithsonian Institution Press.
1980   *The Red Lamp of Incest.* New York: E. P. Dutton.
Frazer, James
1959   *The Golden Bough: A Study in Magic and Religion.* 12 vols.
        3d ed. London: Macmillan and Co. Original 1911–15.
Frisbie, Charlotte J.
1980   "Vocables in Navajo Ceremonial Music." *Ethnomusicology*
        24(3):347–92.
Geertz, Clifford
1966   "Religion as a Cultural System." In Michael Banton, ed.
        Anthropological Approaches to the Study of Religion. London:
        Tavistock.
Goll, Lewis J., S.J.
1940   *Jesuit Missions Among the Sioux.* Saint Francis, S. Dak.:
        Saint Francis Mission.
Greenway, John
1976   *Ethnomusicology.* Minneapolis: Burgess Publishing Co.
Halowell, A. Irving
1955   *Culture and Experience.* Philadelphia: University of Penn-
        sylvania Press.
Halpern, Ida
1976   "On the Interpretation of 'Meaningless–Nonsensical Syl-
        lables' in the Music of the Pacific Northwest Indians."
        Ethnomusicology 20(2):253–71.
Hamilton, W. D.
1971   "Section of Selfish and Altruistic Behavior in Some Ex-
        treme Models." In J. F. Eisenberg and W. S. Dillon, eds.

Man and Beast: Comparative Social Behavior. Washington, D.C.: Smithsonian Institution Press.

Herskovits, Melville J.
1949   Man and His Works. New York: Alfred A. Knopf.

Hockett, Charles F., and Robert Ascher
1964   "The Human Revolution." Current Anthropology 5:135–68.

Holy Rosary Mission
1963   Red Cloud's Dream. Pine Ridge S. Dak.: Red Cloud Indian School.

N.d.   The Story of Red Cloud Indian School. Pine Ridge, S. Dak.: Red Cloud Indian School.

Honigmann, John J.
1954   Culture and Personality. New York: Harper & Row.

Hubert, Henri, and Marcel Mauss
1964   Sacrifice: Its Nature and Function. Chicago: University of Chicago Press. Original 1898.

Hyde, George E.
1956   Red Cloud's Folk. Norman: University of Oklahoma Press.

Hymes, Dell H.
1962   "The Ethnography of Speaking." In T. Gladwin and William C. Sturtevant, eds. Anthropology and Human Behavior. Washington, D.C.: Anthropological Society of Washington.

1965   "Some North Pacific Coast Poems: A Problem in Anthropological Philology." American Anthropologist 67(2):316–41.

1974   Foundations in Sociolinguistics: An Ethnographic Approach. Philadelphia: University of Pennsylvania Press.

Jakobson, Roman
1953   "Result of the Conference of Anthropologists and Linguists, C. Lévi-Strauss, R. Jakobson, C.R. Voeglin, and T. Sebeok." Memoir 8 of the International Journal of American Linguistics. Indiana University Publications in Anthropology and Linguistics.

1960   Concluding Statements: Linguistics and Poetics. In T. Sebeok, ed. Style in Language. Cambridge, Mass.: MIT Press.

Jopling, Carol F. ed.
1971   Art and Aesthetics in Primitive Societies. New York: E. P. Dutton.

Judd, Tedd
1979   Review of Music and the Brain. Brain and Language 7:387–96.

LaBarre, Weston

1970 *The Ghost Dance: The Origins of Religion*. New York: Dell Publishing.

Lane, Michael
1970 *Introduction to Structuralism*. New York: Basic Books.

Langer, Susanne K.
1942 *Philosophy in a New Key*. 3d. ed. Cambridge, Mass.: Harvard University Press.

Leach, Edmund
1958 "Magical Hair." *Journal of the Royal Anthropological Institute* 88(2):147–64.
1961 *Rethinking Anthropology*. London: Athlone Press.
1969 *Genesis as Myth and Other Essays*. London: Jonathan Cape.
1970 *Claude Lévi-Strauss*. New York: Viking Press.
1972 "Buddhism in the Post-Colonial Order in Burma and Ceylon." In S. N. Eisenstadt, ed. *Post-Traditional Societies*. New York: W. W. Norton.

Lenneberg, Eric H., ed.
1964 *New Directions in the Study of Language*. Cambridge, Mass.: MIT Press.

Lenz, Msgr. Paul A.
1979 *An Historical Narrative of the Catholic Sioux Congresses, 1890– 1978*. Pine Ridge, S. Dak.: Holy Rosary Mission.

Lévi-Strauss, Claude.
1962 "Social Structure." In Lévi-Strauss, 1963a.
1963a *Structural Anthropology*. New York: Anchor Books. Original 1958.
1963b *Totemism*. Chicago: University of Chicago Press. Original 1962.
1966 *The Savage Mind*. Chicago: University of Chicago Press. Original 1962.
1969a *The Elementary Structures of Kinship*. Boston: Beacon Press. Original 1949.
1969b *The Raw and the Cooked*. New York: Harper & Row. Original 1964.
1973 *From Honey to Ashes*. New York: Harper & Row. Original 1966.
1976 *Structural Anthropology II*. New York: Basic Books.
1978 *The Origin of Table Manners*. New York: Harper & Row. Original 1968.
1981 *The Naked Man*. New York: Harper & Row. Original 1971.

Lévy-Bruhl, Lucien
1966 *How Natives Think*. New York: Washington Square Press. Original 1926 (English); 1910 (French).

1966a *Primitive Mentality.* Boston: Beacon Press. Original 1923.
1966b *The Soul of the Primitive.* Chicago: Henry Regnery. Original 1928.

Lex, Barbara W.
1979 "The Neurobiology of Ritual Trance." In d'Aquili et al. 1979.

List, George
1968 "The Hopi as Composer and Poet." In P. Crosley–Holland, ed. *Proceedings of the Centennial Workshop on Ethnomusicology* (Government of the Province of British Columbia), 43–51.

Livingstone, F. B.
1973 "Did the Australopithecines Sing?" *Current Anthropology* 14(1–2):12–13.

MacGregor, Gordon
1946 *Warriors Without Weapons.* Chicago: University of Chicago Press.

Mallery, Garrick
1880 *The Sign Language of the North American Indians.* Annual Report of the Bureau of American Ethnology 1 (1879–80):263–552.

Marler, P.
1973 "Developments in the Study of Animal Communication." In Michael W. Fox, ed. *Readings in Ethnology and Comparative Psychology.* Monterey, Calif.: Brooke/Cole Publishing Co.

Mauss, Marcel
1967 *The Gift.* New York: W. W. Norton. Original 1924.

Maynard, Eileen, and Gayla Twiss
1969 "Some Notes on Denominational Preferences Among the Oglalas." *Pine Ridge Research Bulletin* 10:1–6.
1970 *That These People May Live.* Pine Ridge, S. Dak.: U.S. Public Health Service.

Merriam, Alan P.
1967 *Ethnomusicology of the Flathead Indians.* Chicago: Aldine.

Milton, John R.
1972 *Oscar Howe.* Minneapolis: Dillon House.

Nattiez, Jean–Jacques
1975 *Fondements d'une semiologie de la musique.* Paris: Union Généràle d'Éditions.

Needham, Rodney
1972 *Belief, Language, and Experience.* Chicago: University of Chicago Press.

Neihardt, John G.
1932 *Black Elk Speaks.* New York: William Morrow.
Nettl, Bruno
1956 *Music in Primitive Culture.* Cambridge, Mass.: Harvard University Press.
Olson, James C.
1965 *Red Cloud and the Sioux Problem.* Lincoln: University of Nebraska Press.
Otten, Charlotte M.
1971 *Anthropology and Art: Readings in Cross-Cultural Aesthetics.* Garden City, N.Y.: Natural History Press.
Otto, Rudolph
1958 *The Idea of the Holy.* London: Oxford University Press. Original 1924.
Parker, S.
1842 *Journal of an Exploring Tour Beyond the Rocky Mountains.* 3d ed. Ithaca, N.Y.: Mack, Andrus and Woodruff.
Powers, Marla N.
1980 "Menstruation and Reproduction: An Oglala Case." *Signs: The Journal of Women in Culture and Society* 6(1):54–65.
1986 *Oglala Women in Myth, Ritual, and Reality.* Chicago: University of Chicago Press.
Powers, William K.
1961a "The Sioux Omaha Dance." *American Indian Tradition* 8(1):24–33.
1961b "American Indian Music: Contemporary Music and Dance of the Western Sioux." *American Indian Tradition* 7(5):158–65.
1968 "Contemporary Oglala Music and Dance: Pan-Indianism Versus Pan-Tetonism." *Ethnomusicology* 12(3):352–72.
1977 *Oglala Religion.* Lincoln: University of Nebraska Press.
1979 "The Archaic Illusion." *American Indian Art Magazine* 5(1):58–71.
1980 "Plains Indian Music and Dance." In Raymond Wood and Margot Liberty, eds. *Anthropology on the Great Plains.* Lincoln: University of Nebraska Press.
1981a "On Mandalas and Native American World Views." *Current Anthropology* 25:43.
1981b "Bear Facts About Hanto Yo." *Lakota Eyapaha* 5(2):21. Pine Ridge, S.Dak.: Oglala Sioux Community College.
1982 *Yuwipi: Vision and Experience in Oglala Ritual.* Lincoln: University of Nebraska Press.

1985   "Counting Your Blessings: Sacred Numbers and the Structure of Reality. *Zygon* 21(1):75–94.
1986   *Sacred Language: The Nature of Supernatural Discourse in Lakota.* Norman: University of Oklahoma Press.
———— and Marla N. Powers
1984   "Metaphysical Aspects of an Oglala Food System." In Mary Douglass, ed. *Food in the Social Order.* New York: Russell Sage Foundation.

Róheim, Geza
1950   *Psychoanalysis and Culture.* New York: International University Press.

Rossi, Ino, ed.
1974   *The Unconscious in Culture: The Structuralism of Claude Lévi-Strauss in Perspective.* New York: E. P. Dutton.

Ruby, Robert H.
1955   *The Oglala Sioux: Warriors in Transition.* New York: Vantage Press.

Sapir, Edward
1966   *Culture, Language, and Personality.* Berkeley: University of California Press.

Schutz, Alfred
1951   "Making Music Together: A Study in Social Relationship." *Social Research* 18(1):76–97.

Shalvey, Thomas
1979   *Claude Lévi-Strauss: Social Psychotherapy and the Collective Unconscious.* Amherst: University of Massachusetts Press.

Spencer, Herbert
1857   "The Origin and Function of Music." In *Literary Style and Music.* New York: New York Philosophical Library, 1951.

Steinmetz, Paul, S.J.
1969   "Explanation of the Sacred Pipe as a Prayer Instrument." *Pine Ridge Research Bulletin* 10:20–25.
1980   *Pipe, Bible and Peyote Among the Oglala Lakota: A Study in Religious Identity.* Stockholm: Motala.

Swann, Brian, ed.
1983   *Smoothing the Ground: Essays on Native American Oral Literature.* Berkeley: University of California Press.

Tomkins, William
1969   *Indian Sign Language.* New York: Dover Publications.

Torrey, E. Fuller
1972   *The Mind Game: Witchdoctors and Psychiatrists.* New York: Emerson Hall Publishers.

Trivers, R. L.

1971   "The Evolution of Reciprocal Altruism." *Quarterly Review of Biology* 46(4): 35–57.

1972   "Parental Investment and Sexual Selection." In Bernard Campbell, ed. *Sexual Selection and the Descent of Man.* Chicago: Aldine.

Turner, Victor W.

1969   *The Ritual Process.* Chicago: Aldine.

1985   "Body, Brain, and Culture." *Zygon: Journal of Religion and Science.* 18 (September): 221–45.

Utley, Robert M.

1963   *The Last Days of the Sioux Nation.* New Haven, Conn.: Yale University Press.

Van Gennep, Arnold

1960   *The Rites of Passage.* Chicago: University of Chicago Press. Original 1909.

Wachsmann, Klaus P.

1971   "Universal Perspectives in Music." *Ethnomusicology* 15(3): 381–84.

Walker. J.R.

1917   "The Sun Dance and Other Ceremonies in the Oglala Division of Teton–Dakota." *American Museum of Natural History Anthropological Papers* 16: 51–221.

Wallace, Anthony F. C.

1956   "Revitalization Movements." *American Anthropologist* 58: 264–81.

1961   *Culture and Personality.* New York: Random House.

Williams, B. J.

1981   "A Critical Review of Models in Sociobiology." *Annual Review of Anthropology* 10: 163–92.

Wilson, E. O.

1975   *Sociobiology: The New Synthesis.* Cambridge, Mass.: Harvard University Press.

Wissler, Clark

1971   *Red Man Reservations.* New York: Collier Books. Original 1938.

Zimmerly, David

1969   "On Being an Ascetic: Personal Document of a Sioux Medicine Man." *Pine Ridge Research Bulletin* 10: 46–69.

INDEX